The Aviation History of Greater Riverside

The Aviation History of Greater Riverside

Marge Bitetti & Tony Bitetti

The History Press

Published by The History Press
Charleston, SC 29403
www.historypress.net

First published 2013

Manufactured in the United States

ISBN 978.1.60949.630.2

Library of Congress CIP data applied for.

CONTENTS

FOREWORD

Riverside County is home to a rich cultural history and, most notably, a proud tradition of aviation. From the many general aviation airports to the historic March Joint Air Reserve Base, Riverside is an alluring destination for aviation enthusiasts and historians.

Riverside's history is filled with remarkable stories, such as the creation of the March Air Force Base. In the early years of the twentieth century, the United States Congress instructed U.S. generals to prepare America for entry into World War I by putting "the Yankee punch into the war by building an army in the air." Out of that order, a base was commissioned at Alessandro Field in Riverside, California. This field is one of the gems of Riverside and is critical to American military capabilities. It has supported as many as eighty-five thousand troops at the height of activity and was the hub of West Coast deployments to the Middle East.

As part of the community effort to recognize the proud history of aviation, the March Field Air Museum is now home to the Distinguished Flying Cross Memorial. The Distinguished Flying Cross honors members of the armed forces who demonstrate extraordinary heroism during aerial flight. The March Air Field Museum has become the nationwide symbol for the commemoration of Distinguished Flying Cross recipients; these are individuals who have made many incredible sacrifices in their service to our nation.

March Joint Air Reserve Base and the March Field Air Museum are just two examples of the importance of Riverside County to U.S. aviation explored in *The Aviation History of Greater Riverside*. Marge and Tony Bitetti have greatly contributed to the chronology of Southern California through excellent collections of local narratives, and this book will certainly be remembered as a wonderful addition to local history as it highlights the remarkable contributions that Riverside County has made to U.S. aviation.

Congressman Ken Calvert
Forty-fourth Congressional District

ACKNOWLEDGEMENTS

Working on this book has been an educational and memorable experience. Thanks are fitting to so many people who helped make this book possible. We learned so much about the brave men who saw the possibilities and acted on their dreams to make aviation history in Riverside a reality. Special thanks to the following people, who assisted in some way to make this book possible:

Tony Haraman and Ralph Cooper
From the Corona Airport, City of Corona: Richard Brodeur and Bob and Meta Suko
From Riverside Municipal Airport: Mark Ripley, director; Corinne Parker, Hank Schmel; Pete Downes; and Bud Ukes
From Skylark Field: Larry Perkins
Author Kim Jarrell Johnson
From Flabob Airport: Roman Warren Jr. and family, Don Madariaga, John D. Lyon, the Tom Wathen Center and Kathy Rohm
From Banning: Cheri McRae
From Perris Valley Airport: Melanie Peschio and the Conatser family
From March Air Reserve Base and March Field Air Museum: Patricia Korzec, who granted access to the March Field Air Museum, and also Michelle Sifuentes and Bruce Ward
Congressman Ken Calvert

This section would not be complete without a word of thanks to the brave barnstormers. Thanks to Roman Warren and Flavio Madariaga, and their wives, who lived to create the history that was an inspiration to countless people who followed.

OVERVIEW OF RIVERSIDE

Spanish Days

In 1774, Juan Bautista de Anza led a group through the territory to discover a new land route from southern Mexico to Alta, California. They settled in what is known today as Riverside. The location was named Valley of Paradise. In the 1930s, to commemorate de Anza's visit, a twenty-foot statue of him was erected at the corner of Market and Fourteenth Streets through private donations and a federal grant from the Works Progress Administration (WPA).

Riverside Established

The city of Riverside is the county seat of Riverside County, which covers 7,208 square miles and is bordered by Orange County on the west; La Paz County, Arizona, on the east; San Diego County on the southwest; Imperial County on the southeast; and San Bernardino County on the north.

Riverside gets its name from its proximity to the Santa Ana River. The river, which runs through San Bernardino, Los Angeles, Orange and Riverside Counties, is the largest river in Southern California and was important to early settlements in Riverside. The city of Riverside was established in the early 1870s by John Wesley North, an abolitionist from Tennessee. North was a statesman and later became a U.S. senator in Nevada. North and some associates founded a community in Northfield, Minnesota, in 1855. He later moved west to California and was joined by associates who helped in the establishment of Riverside.

North was a skillful man. When he was only fifteen, he started teaching school. In 1833, he became a licensed preacher. He later studied law and was admitted to the New York State bar in 1845. He died in 1890 at the age of seventy-five and is buried in Evergreen Cemetery in Riverside.

Citrus Industry

Citrus crops helped Riverside gain fame and fortune. In 1873, Eliza Tibbets introduced seedless oranges to the city by planting two trees in her garden. Since she was not connected to any main water supply, it is believed that she used her dishwater to nourish the trees. The first fruit produced by these trees grew in 1875–76. The fruit was known as the Washington navel orange. These new oranges were publicly displayed at a fair in 1879. The oranges were widely praised for their shape, size, color, texture and flavor. Tibbets sold cuttings from her orange trees to local nurseries. The trees thrived in the Southern California climate, and the navel orange industry grew rapidly. The growth of the orange industry led to the boom of the California citrus industry, which is commemorated in the landscapes and exhibits of the California Citrus State Historic Park in Riverside. By 1882, there were more than half a million citrus trees in California, almost half of which were in Riverside. The development of refrigerated railroad cars and innovative irrigation systems established Riverside as the wealthiest city per capita by 1895.

The Washington navel orange was a $30 million per year industry in Riverside by 1917. The citrus industry increased to $67 million by 1933; it grew from 1.0 million boxes of oranges in 1887 to 65.5 million boxes in 1944. The citrus boom was not harmed by the Depression and continued to grow.

Many people relocated to Riverside for the warm, dry climate and to leave behind the harsh winters on the East Coast. In 1905, the *Riverside Daily Press* reported that a brochure was created to send to the people on the East Coast to promote the area.

The Mission Inn

All the fame from the citrus industry brought more people to Riverside. It was fitting that a hotel be built to accommodate the visitors. Christopher Columbus Miller built the Glenwood Tavern, which was later known as the Mission Inn. The Miller family moved from Wisconsin to settle in Riverside and join Christopher Columbus Miller, their father. The first structure was located at the corner of Seventh Street (now Mission Avenue) and Main Street. The building had twelve cottages. In 1888, the building became known as the Glenwood Inn. The property was owned by Frank Miller's father, who sold the property to Frank.

It was Frank Miller's dream to create a spacious hotel on the land. He selected the Mission Revival style for his hotel, which was inspired by the California missions left along the coast by Franciscan friars in the sixteenth and seventeenth centuries. Construction of the new hotel began in 1902. Miller gained financial backing from Henry Huntington, and architect Arthur Benton was hired. The Glenwood Inn became known as the famous Mission Inn, which was favored by presidents, royalty and movie stars. Inside was a special chair made for the sizable president William Howard Taft. The Mission Inn Hotel and Spa now has 238 rooms and suites and has hosted ten presidents. President Theodore Roosevelt and Richard Nixon, who held his wedding at the hotel, are just a few of the notable guests.

Frank Miller successfully managed the Mission Inn until his death in 1935. The improvement in air travel and the Great Depression affected the inn. After Frank Miller's death, his daughter Allis and son-in-law DeWitt Hutchings took on management of the hotel. For a brief period of time, the hotel served as housing for students at the University of California–Riverside. In 1956, the Miller family sold the hotel. It is now owned by Duane R. Roberts, chairman, president and CEO of the Historic Mission Inn Corporation, headquartered in Newport Beach, California.

For over twenty years, the owners of the Mission Inn and Spa, Duane and Kelly Roberts, have hosted the largest collection of holiday lights in the nation. From the Friday after Thanksgiving until early January, visitors are greeted with more than 3.6 million lights and displays transforming the hotel into a magical holiday land. The annual Festival of Lights has become a seasonal tradition for countless visitors from near and far.

The Fliers' Wall

In 1931, Miller built the St. Francis Chapel, which was a fitting place for weddings and celebrations. The chapel contains a gold-leafed Reyes Altar and Louis Comfort Tiffany stained-glass windows. Also in the chapel is a tribute to pilots. On the famous Fliers' Wall, several aviation greats are remembered, including the following:

Captain Eddie Rickenbacker
General H.H. "Hap" Arnold
Major General Robert Olds
Amelia Earhart
James H. Doolittle
General Hoyt S. Vandenberg
John K. Northrop
General Curtis LeMay
Jacqueline Cochran
Charles Lindbergh
Brigadier General Chuck Yeager
Mercury Astronaut and Senator John Glenn

Eddie Rickenbacker was a member of the Ninety-fourth Aero Pursuit Squadron, a group of fliers active during World War I. Before the war, Rickenbacker was an internationally known racecar driver. After World War I, he went on to become president of Eastern Airlines. On March 20, 1942, Rickenbacker was honored at the Mission Inn. He was the fifty-seventh flier to have copper wings added to the famous Fliers' Wall. Later that same year, Rickenbacker was on an inspection trip for the United States when his plane crashed into the Pacific Ocean. Rickenbacker and six others survived on rubber rafts for twenty-four days before being rescued.

The pilots are honored with 154 pairs of ten-inch copper wings that are displayed on the wall. Missing in action (MIA) and prisoners of war (POWs) are remembered with copper wings wrapped in barbed wire.

Airfield Created

The United States declared war on Germany, entered World War I on April 6, 1917, and passed the Selective Service Act on May 10. Germany bombed London on June 12, and the next day, the deadliest German air raid on London during World War I was carried out by Gotha G bombers, resulting in 162 deaths (including 46 children) and 432 injuries. The following day, more than 100 people were killed in East London by a German air attack. French pilot Georges Guynemer shot down his fifty-fourth German aircraft on September 6. Love Field in Dallas, Texas, was opened on October 19. The first U.S. pilot to down an enemy airplane was Stephen W. Thompson on February 5, 1918, and Douglas Campbell became the first U.S. ace pilot (after he shot down his fifth German plane) on April 14.

An aviation committee was created in Riverside. The committee included Riverside attorney W.A. Purington; George Sarau; Lieutenant George Price, an ROTC instructor at high schools and colleges; and, most importantly, Frank Miller. In 1917, Miller, Hiram Johnson and other prominent Californians were successful in getting approval for an army air strip to be built at Alessandro Field. The field was to be used by aviators flying on cross-country flights from Rockwell Field in San Diego. A parade was held in 1918 to announce that an army flying field would soon be located in Riverside. On March 20, 1918, Alessandro Field became March Field.

Airplanes were becoming more prominent in the news. S. Potter became the first U.S. pilot to shoot down a German seaplane on March 19, 1918. Manfred von Richthofen (aka the Red Baron) shot down his seventy-ninth and eightieth victims, marking his final victories before his death the following day, on April 21. The first airmail postal service was inaugurated between New York, Philadelphia and Washington, D.C., on May 15. The first airplane bombing raid by an American unit occurred in France on June 12. The first flight between the Hawaiian Islands occurred on June 28.

On November 10, 1918, the Western Union cable office in North Sydney, Nova Scotia, received a top-secret coded message from Europe (that would be sent to Ottawa, Ontario, Canada and Washington, D.C.). that said all fighting would cease on land, at sea and in the air. World War I ended at 11:00 a.m. on the Western Front on November 11, 1918—Armistice Day.

BARNSTORMING

Barnstorming became a popular form of entertainment throughout the United States in the 1920s. It also found its way west to Riverside. It could be considered an early form of commercial aviation, but the first commercial flight in history occurred in the United States on January 1, 1914, three years before the United States entered the First World War. The flight took place between St. Petersburg and Tampa, Florida, flying a total of twenty-three minutes between the two cities, separated by twenty-one miles of bay waters. The plane maintained an altitude of fifteen feet across the open waters of the bay rather than a high arc like one would see in today's flights. The plane was a Benoist XIV, a two-seater with a very small flight deck. It was piloted by Tony Jannus.

There was an auction held for this inaugural flight between the cities, with people bidding large amounts of money for the only passenger seat on the aircraft. The winner was Mr. Abram Pheil, who paid the price of $400, which would be over $5,000 in today's currency. Mr. Pheil was the former mayor of St. Petersburg and was very eager to take this first flight of the St. Petersburg–Tampa Air Line.

While this flight was a historic event, it wasn't until after the Second World War that commercial aviation came down in price. The United States had created manufacturing plants that were capable of making commercial aircraft affordable enough to allow for air travel for everyone. This was a big change from the beginning of the aviation era. With planes being able to be mass-produced, more companies could compete with one another for customers and destination cities. Airports began to spring up all over the country, allowing people to go from city to city with more ease than ever before.

All of this was made possible by that flight in 1914 by Tony Jannus in his Benoist airplane, with his passenger by his side. Without that historic flight and the buzz generated by the auction for that seat, the idea of flight as a way to travel might have taken even longer to develop.

By the early 1920s, barnstorming stunt pilots were performing tricks with airplanes. Barnstorming became the first major form of civil aviation in the history of flight. The term also applied to pilots who flew throughout the country selling airplane rides, an early form of commercial aviation, which usually consisted of operating from a farmer's field for a day or two before moving on. "Barnstorming season" ran from early spring until after the harvest and county fairs in the fall. Since the area surrounding Riverside was largely agricultural during those years, it attracted many barnstormers who took advantage of the curiosity of the crowds of people who would visit their shows.

In the 1920s, barnstorming gained popularity. Many adventurous pilots earned their livings by barnstorming across the country. Famous aviator Charles Lindbergh was once a barnstormer. Roman Warren was well known in the Riverside area for his barnstorming adventures. Well-known barnstormers included Roscoe Turner, Wiley Post, female pilot Pancho Barnes and the first licensed African American female pilot, Bessie Coleman.

During World War I, the United States had manufactured a significant number of Curtiss JN-4s (called Jennys) to train its military aviators. Almost every U.S. airman had learned to fly using the plane. After the war, the U.S. federal government sold off the surplus materiel, including the Jennys, for a fraction of its initial value (the $5,000 purchase price of a Jenny could be reduced to as low as $200). This permitted many of the servicemen, who were already familiar with the JN-4s, to purchase their own planes. The Standard J-1 biplane, almost identical in appearance to the Curtiss aircraft, also frequently found itself similarly available.

There were many small companies that got started building planes, but many went out of business almost as soon as they opened. It was a time when pilots performed various activities just for the opportunity to fly. Some pilots flew the mail; others found work as barnstormers, and a few even took to the sky as smugglers.

Combined with the lack of federal aviation regulations at the time, these factors allowed barnstorming to flourish during the postwar era.

Most barnstorming shows started with a pilot or a team of pilots flying over a small rural town to attract the attention of the local inhabitants. They would then land at a local farm (hence the name "barnstorming") and negotiate with the farmer for the use of one of his fields as a temporary runway from which to stage an air show and offer airplane rides to customers. After obtaining a base of operation, the pilot or group of aviators would "buzz" the village, dropping handbills offering airplane rides for a small fee and advertising the daring feats that would be performed. Crowds would follow the planes to the field, purchase rides and watch the show.

Barnstormers became skilled doing aerobatic stunts, performing anything that would draw a crowd. Some of the maneuvers included dives, spins and loops. Sometimes wing walkers would perform with the barnstormers, walking cautiously on the wing of the plane while it was in flight.

Although barnstormers often worked in solitude or in very small teams, some also put together large "flying circuses" with several planes and stunt people. These acts employed promoters to book shows in towns ahead of time. They were the largest and most organized of all the barnstorming acts.

One early barnstorming pilot well known in Riverside was Roman Warren, sometimes known as the "Cowboy Aviator." He was an early manager of what would become Flabob Air Field.

In November 1918, after the end of World War I, civil aviation in the United States was primarily unregulated and made up of barnstormers, who operated inexpensive military surplus aircraft from city to city, often landing in farm fields on the outskirts of towns, as airports were scarce at that time. These traveling aviators offered airplane rides and aerobatic flight demonstrations and frequently performed impromptu air shows for the townsfolk, charging whatever the local economic conditions would allow. As a result, mechanics and early flight instructors moved around with the aircraft and had no established business in any one location.

With passage of the Air Commerce Act of 1926 and its resulting requirements for the licensing of pilots, aircraft maintenance requirements and regulations in training standards, the transient nature of civil aviation was cut back. The pilots and mechanics who made their livings on the road began establishing permanent businesses, termed fixed-base operations (FBOs), at the growing number of airports appearing throughout the United States as a way to distinguish permanent businesses from the transient businesses common prior to 1926.

Today, fixed-base operations at airports supply a wide range of aeronautical needs. Pilots can rely on FBOs for fuel, air charter services, training and classes for pilots. FBOs often offer aircraft for sale or rent and hangars for housing airplanes. Often, pilots can find repair facilities at FBOs or maintenance for planes. Unique services that are often available at FBOs include aerial photography, crop dusting and aerial advertising.

FBOs have provided many services for pilots and ensure flight safety through the services that are provided.

Within the United States, the Federal Aviation Administration (FAA) regulates some activities that might compose an FBO, such as authorization or repair stations, flight training and air taxi/air carrier services, but the overarching term "FBO" has no regulatory standards through the federal government. The United States Department of Transportation, in cooperation with the FAA, has the duty of establishing minimum standards for commercial aeronautical activities and recommends implementation of these standards by the airport operator or agency.

Although barnstorming thrived during the first half of the 1920s, by 1927, competition between the acts demanded more and more dangerous tricks. A rash of highly publicized accidents forced the implementation of new safety regulations that resulted in the demise of barnstorming.

A need to protect the public, and in response to political pressure by local pilots who were upset at barnstormers stealing their customers, the federal government enacted several laws to begin regulating fledgling civil aviation. The laws included safety standards, requirements for a flying license and specifications that were nearly impossible for barnstormers to meet, as well as restrictions on how low in altitude certain tricks could be performed (making it harder for spectators to see what was happening). The military also stopped selling Jennys in the late 1920s, and this, combined with the regulations, made it too difficult for barnstormers to continue to make a living. However, some pilots continued to wander the country giving rides as late as the fall of 1941.

Some modern pilots flying restored vintage aircraft or accurate reproduction aircraft of vintage design continue the barnstorming tradition today and offer open-cockpit biplane rides to the public from a handful of airports around the country.

THE BIRTH OF AIRPORTS

Shortly after the Wright brothers' memorable flight in 1903, people began to think that soon every home would have a plane. General aviation or civilian aviation did not become popular until the mid-1920s. The dream of flying became so popular that Americans used the expression the "Winged Gospel" to describe the almost religious romanticism people had for aviation. Author and historian Joseph Corn described the excitement with airplanes and the new technology in his book, *The Winged Gospel.* There was a belief that the airplane would change the world. There were many who also thought that the airplane was destined to become as common as the automobile.

In the 1920s, airplanes were used for crop-dusting and aerial land surveying. Glen Curtiss, a rival to the Wright brothers, began to manufacture planes. These were purchased by the wealthy and by exhibition pilots. Just before World War I, Clyde Cessna opened an aircraft company. Cessna's goal was to build inexpensive planes for personal use. The lower costs of planes helped to bring more pilots to the sport. Popular in the 1920s and '30s was the OX-5 engine. Although these engines were cheaper, they were large and required a larger aircraft. The most expensive part of the aircraft was the engine.

In the early years immediately following the flight of the Wright brothers, there were no pilot's licenses. The Aero Club of America, which started primarily as a social club, was organized in 1905. It issued the first pilot's license to Glenn Curtiss in 1911. The Aero Club of America was established by members of the Automobile Club of America, including Charles Glidden, David Morris, John R. O'Rourke, Augustus Post and Homer Hedge, who served as the first president of the organization. In 1923, the club became known as the National Aeronautic Association.

Pilot's licenses were not required until after World War I. The interest in flying created the need for smaller airports, where new pilots could land. Many open crop fields yielded the way for planes to land. The lower cost of planes helped to put more pilots in the sky.

During World War I, planes matured. The planes that were used for the military had to stand up to combat and maintenance in times of war. A 1915 issue of *Flying* magazine stated that World War I was "the last great war in history," citing that airplanes would promote peace and harmony and end national rivalries that led to war.

After the war, there was a surplus of planes that could be purchased for a nominal price. This created more pilots and fostered the advent of the age of the barnstormers. In 1926, Henry Ford introduced the "Ford Flying Flivver." This plane held only one person but created a keen interest in aviation. A crash of a Flivver in 1928 killed the pilot and caused Ford to lose interest in aviation.

In 1929, the Aeronca C-2 was introduced. It sold for under $2,000 and was powered by a thirty-six-horsepower engine that was produced by Aeronca. An interesting story was recorded in St. Louis, Missouri, when men loaded a cow into a plane, milked the animal in the air and then dropped small containers of milk with tiny parachutes across the city. Such stunts helped to promote the public's fascination with aviation. Soon, people wanted to get married in the sky while flying over a city. One woman was reported to even give birth high in the sky to a girl whom she named Aerogene Airleen. The couple chartered a Fokker tri-motor and flew high above Miami, Florida. Present for the birth on the airplane were a doctor, nurse, the copilot and the baby's maternal grandmother.

About the same time, "Cowboy Aviator" Roman Warren was attracting attention in Riverside, California, with his flying circus and barnstorming adventures.

In the 1930s, Eugene Vidal, who was in charge of the Bureau of Air Commerce during Franklin Delano Roosevelt's administration, felt that the nation needed a low-cost, all-metal plane with a price of about $700. At the time, new automobiles cost between $300 and $500. Overall, this plan was not a success, but it created a buzz that aviation might be within the reach of everyone.

In order to increase the number of pilots in America, the Civil Aeronautics Authority sponsored a pilot training program. This program did cause an increase in the number of pilots in the United States. Aviation services increased for crop dusting, which was important in the South to help eliminate the boll weevil. Planes were also useful for the treatment of forest land and the advent of the business traveler.

By the end of the 1930s, there were several affordable engines being built for small aircraft. A Piper J-3 Cub sold for just under $1,000. As aircraft costs got lower, there were an increased number of pilots and a growing need for places to land aircraft. This progress helped to foster airports such as Banning, Riverside-Arlington and Skylark Field in Riverside County, California. The prophecy of the "Winged Gospel" was rapidly spreading across the nation.

An article in a 1930s issue of *Harper's Weekly* was titled "An Airplane in Every Garage." People believed that as the horseless carriage had replaced the bicycle and the horse-drawn carriage, the airplane would soon replace the automobile. In 1934, newspaper publisher William Randolph Hearst used his papers to create the largest model plane–building organization in the United States. The organization, which was named the Junior Birdmen of America, was open to all boys and girls ages ten through twenty-one. The cost of membership was one dime. The goal was to promote air education in the youth. The motto of the organization was: "Today, pilots of models. Tomorrow, model pilots." Some schools even included aviation material in their curriculum. The program ran with the support of the newspaper until 1937. After 1937, the organization ran independent of the paper, with offices in the RCA building in Rockefeller Center, New York City, and officials such as Captain E.V. Rickenbacker. Membership became twenty-five cents, and stories were available in a monthly magazine instead of the daily and weekly newspaper.

During World War II, private aviation was grounded. But many pilots found a way to be in the clouds by joining the Civil Air Patrol. Members of the Civil Air Patrol flew over the coastline looking for enemy submarines. Other Civil Air Patrol members flew over the forestland and were spotters for forest fires or flew humanitarian missions to drop supplies to areas of the country devastated by floods, fires or tornados.

Most small private airports were closed during the war years. For example, Flabob Airport was not active during World War II, but it became a hub of activity when it was purchased after the war.

The ERCO Ercoupe 415 first went on sale in 1941. It was a two-seat plane. During World War II, the planes were used by the Civil Air Patrol to spot German submarines. Production of the plane resumed after the war. It was thought that thousands of men and women who trained as pilots during the war would enjoy flying in peacetime. In 1946, 4,311 Ercoupe model 415-Cs were produced. They sold in the United States for $2,665. One of the outlets for the sale of the planes was the men's department of the New York Macy's department store.

By the 1950s, the age of air travel had come to blossom. More people began to use airplanes for business travel, as well as for vacation travel. Despite earlier predictions, most homes did not have access to their own planes. World War II showed the importance of aviation for the military. According to historian Joseph Corn, "Aviation would continue to advance but the winged gospel theory had faded." However, there was enough interest in aviation to merit the advancement of small regional airports such as Corona Airport and Riverside Municipal.

Following World War II, many of the aircraft companies that had been successful in the early 1920s and '30s went out of business. From the 1950s through the '70s, top names of manufacturers included Piper, Cessna and Beech. There was a transition from fabric-covered planes to planes made of metal. By 1920, the market for personal flying had peaked.

BANNING MUNICIPAL AIRPORT

FAA Identifier:	BNG
Lat./Long.:	33-55-21.2000N / 116-51-03.5000W 33-55.353333N / 116-51.058333W 33.9225556 / -116.8509722 (estimated)
Elevation:	2222 ft. / 677.3 m. (surveyed)
Variation:	14E (1985)
From City:	1 mile SE of Banning, CA
Time zone:	UTC-7 (UTC-8 during Standard Time)
Zip Code:	92220

The city of Banning was incorporated in 1913. Initially, it was a stagecoach stop for travelers going from Los Angeles to Arizona. The city has scenic views from the two tallest mountain peaks in Southern California: Mount San Gorgonio and Mount San Jacinto. It was a logical spot for the development of aviation.

In 1911, eight years after the first flight by the Wright brothers, the Hearst Transcontinental Flight Derby—organized by William Randolph Hearst—sponsored a $50,000 prize for the first pilot to complete a flight across the United States in fewer than thirty days. Two notable pilots who competed in the race were Calbraith "Cal" P. Rodgers and Robert C. Fowler. Rodgers started his flight in Sheepshead, New York, and Fowler started his flight in San Francisco. Fowler's destination was Jacksonville, Florida.

Rodgers was one of the first pilots to purchase a Wright Flyer. He started his journey with only sixty hours of flight experience. The plane could reach speeds of just fifty to sixty miles per hour and had no instruments or gauges. Rodgers could depend only on line-of-sight navigating to take him across the continent. Along his four-thousand-mile journey, he crashed over fifteen times and made several visits to various hospitals. There were no airports or aircraft mechanics along the way and no air navigation maps, control towers or beacons to warn of hazards or to guide the pilot. Pilots had to follow railroad tracks, recognize landmarks and talk with local people during periods on the ground.

Both pilots flew in the area above Banning in the San Gorgonio Pass. Fowler landed his biplane to repair one of the engines. Fowler was also flying in a Wright biplane equipped with a Cole Motor Car Company engine. Before flying, Fowler drove race cars and won several events between 1903 and 1911. He landed in south Beaumont on land that was known as the Stewart Ranch. After starting his flight on October 22, 1911, he finally reached Florida on January 10, 1912. His flight took him 112 days. He was the first to start the journey and the last to finish.

In November, Rodgers landed his plane a little south of Banning. He needed to stop due to engine trouble. He was forced to land a second time at the same Stewart Ranch where Fowler had landed before him. Rodgers made seventy stops and had numerous injuries during his eighty-six hours in the air before he finally reached his destination in Pasadena, California. Although Rodgers was nineteen days too late to receive the prize money, he never gave up until he finished the first transcontinental airplane flight. He died in a plane crash a few months later, on April 3, 1912, in Long Beach, California. Since Hearst had specified that the flight must be done in fewer than thirty days, the prize expired in November 1911 with no winner.

Beginning in 1918, pilots from March Field often landed their planes at Stewart Ranch. Where the planes landed was determined by what part of the ranch was planted and what section was being plowed.

Banning is a small town of about twenty-three thousand people in the Southern California desert. It is located one hundred miles east of Los Angeles and twenty-five miles west of Palm Springs. It sits in a desert valley between the San Bernardino and Little San Bernardino Mountains and offers views of Mount San Gorgonio to the north and Mount San Jacinto to the south.

Taking off from the Banning Airport. *Courtesy Cheri McRae.*

The airport is located on the southeast corner of the city and is used primarily for general aviation. In other words, this is an airport where pilots can fly small, private planes with propellers. It has a 5,200-foot-long runway. Pilots wishing to fly planes into this airport should contact the City of Banning.

The airport was established in 1927 by the Banning Kiwanis Club. The club obtained options on seventy acres of Southern Pacific Railroad land east of downtown Banning. The field was named Rodgers Airport in memory of Cal Rodgers and his landing in Banning in the first transcontinental flight of 1911. In 1928, a Fourth of July celebration was held to help raise money for the airport. There were fifty-three lots plotted on the land that sold for $100 each. Ownership of the airport was then transferred to the City of Banning. Events during the Fourth of July celebration included a nonstop race from Banning to Los Angeles, balloons, parachutes and auto races.

In neighboring Beaumont, there were several airstrips used for landings and takeoffs, but there were no provisions for plane storage or fueling. In the early 1920s, there was a dirt airfield north of Ramsey and east of Highland Springs. Pilots from March Field used to land their planes on this airstrip. In

Power-generating windmills in the background near Banning Airport. *Courtesy Cheri McRae.*

Landing at Banning Airport, established in the 1940s. *Courtesy Cheri McRae.*

the 1930s and '40s, there was oil exploration in Beaumont near California Avenue, and there was a small airstrip that was used for this oil operation. In the late part of the 1950s, an airport was named in the southern portion of Beaumont just north of the present Interstate 10 Freeway.

Today, Banning Municipal Airport covers approximately 141 acres. The airport averages twenty-five aircraft operations per day and has one runway running east to west. With three gates total, the airport has no tower but does have offices, fuel stations and hangars.

CORONA MUNICIPAL AIRPORT

FAA Identifier:	AJO
Lat./Long.:	33-53-51.5547N / 117-36-08.7831W
	33-53.859245N / 117-36.146385W
	33.8976541 / -117.6024398
	(estimated)
Elevation:	533 ft. / 162.5 m. (surveyed)
Variation:	14E (1980)
From City:	3 miles NW of Corona, CA
Time Zone:	UTC-8 (UTC-7 during Daylight Saving Time)
Zip Code:	92880

The city of Corona is located approximately forty-five miles southeast of Los Angeles in western Riverside County. Corona is ideally situated at the base of the mountainous Cleveland National Forest. The city was originally called South Riverside, but in 1896, the residents voted to change the name to Corona (Spanish for "crown") in honor of the circular roads in the center of the city. The Corona Foothill Lemon Company, which was established on June 15, 1911, became the largest lemon ranch in all of California. For a time, Corona became known as the "Lemon Capital of the World."

In about 1925, there was a flying field located at the Parkridge Country Club, northeast of Corona. The surface was dirt and pretty rough. Before

This aerial view of Corona Airport shows how the area has developed. *Courtesy City of Corona.*

1930, barnstormers came to the area to sell rides. One of them operated a flying service approximately where Sixth Street now meets the 91 Freeway. By 1920, several local residents, including Dr. Denver Roos, Glen James and Harry M. Johnson Sr., had made a landing strip in a dirt field owned by the Kuster brothers, owners of Kuster & Waterbury Sand, Gravel and Excavating. The location was near where the 91 and 15 Freeways now intersect, near the KUBC (KWRM) radio towers.

In 1945, George Dober established an airport in what is known as the Home Gardens area off Magnolia Avenue, south of what was then the Hickory Restaurant and is now Angels Sports Bar. When the property was sold, he relocated to the former Kuster field on property leased by Scott Thursby, then called Thursby Field Airport. The address was East Parkridge Avenue 1W Kuster. In 1947, Los Angeles Airways, the world's first scheduled helicopter airline, started carrying airmail and air express into Corona. The heliport was located on Grand Avenue, approximately where St. Edward's Catholic Church now sits.

Other known airports were in the Corona area in the late 1940s. A dirt strip was located in Norco on the northeast corner of Second and Mountain. Among those involved were Red Rickoff and Bob Beets, a former P51 pilot. There was an air strip at the south end of the property owned by the

In the early 1960s, when the 91 Freeway was built, it forced the airport to move to its present site. *Courtesy City of Corona.*

Norconian Hotel. There was another field in Norco that was a dirt strip located a few blocks north of Sixth Street and California. John Macelroy had a dirt strip approximately where the Serfas Golf Course is now located. It was near Cherry Hills Court and Mountain View. It was described as being at the end of Ontario Street. There was also a private air field built by a contractor near Mangular Avenue. Glen Ivy Hot Springs in Corona had a short runway that wasn't easy to fly into or out of.

Thursby Field, which was on leased land, was bought by the City of Corona on January 4, 1956. By 1958, California had 13 percent of the nation's pilots and only 7 percent of the nation's airports.

In January 1958, discussions were held with the California Aeronautics Commission for the relocation of the airport from Thursby Field. The City Airport Committee—consisting of Joe Greer, Gene Mazwell and Scott Thursby—had recommended land along the east edge of the old city dump, which now lies east of the 15 Freeway and south of Magnolia. The property was already owned by the city, and there were ongoing negotiations with Riverside County concerning the dump.

In February 1958, the estimated cost of installing a 100-foot-long landing strip at the dump site was $3,300. In March, ground and aerial inspections were conducted of several possible sites. The field representative from the California Aeronautics Commission nixed the dump site. It fell short of the requirements of a runway 3,000 to 3,500 feet long, although it could accommodate 100 feet wide. Mountainous terrain and lease negotiations for the dump with the county were all obstacles. The representatives favored the site owned by the federal government in the Prado Basin. The land had four years left on a five-year lease to Exchange Lemon Products Company and was known as the Lilybridge Ranch. Also in March, Olympic Rock Products, Inc., said that Thursby Field could continue but was subject to a thirty-day notice of cancellation by the company. Plans to move the airport were put on hold.

In 1960, when Corona Airport was getting started, John F. Kennedy won the presidential election with Lyndon B. Johnson as his running mate. The margin was very slim, with 113,000 votes out of 68.3 million. The average price for a home was $12,700, and inflation was at 1.46 percent. The Flintstones were on television for the first time. A loaf of bread was twenty cents, gasoline was twenty-five cents per gallon and the average cost of a new car was $2,600. The average wage in this year was $4,743, and a teacher's salary was at $5,174, with the minimum wage at $1 an hour. Transistor radios were new on the scene and were a must-have for every teenager.

When the 91 Freeway was built, it forced the airport to make a move. The runway was south of the present location, approximately where Airport Drive is now located. It had one FBO at the northeast end of the field. Planes were tied down on the north edge of the field. Gene Maxwell was asked to test the runway and was the first to land on it while it was still being graded. In May 1961, the 91 Freeway was completed in Corona. In the same year, there were 238,000 air traffic operations in Riverside County.

During the cold war, Corona students participated in the Crusade for Freedom. The Crusade for Freedom was a fund drive to bring the message of freedom to Eastern Europe beyond the Iron Curtain.

The Lockheed U2—a single-engine, very high-altitude (seventy thousand feet over thirteen miles) reconnaissance aircraft that was operated by the United States Air Force (USAF)—was introduced in 1960. On May 1 of that year, pilot Francis Gary Powers was shot down by a Russian SA-2 Guideline surface-to-air missile over Soviet airspace while he was photographing ICBM sites in and around Sverdlovsk and Plesetsk. The United States denied that the aircraft was a covert surveillance aircraft, but the Soviet Union produced its intact remains and surviving pilot Powers, plus photos of military bases in Russia taken by the pilot. On August 19, Powers was sentenced to three years' imprisonment and seven years' hard labor for espionage on the Soviet Union. On February 10, 1962, Powers and American student Frederic Pryor were exchanged for Soviet KGB colonel Vilyam Fisher. The U2 incident and the subsequent bad publicity for the United States helped accelerate the use of spy satellites for reconnaissance by the United States and the Soviet Union during the 1960s and the cold war.

In the early 1960s, housing developments were just beginning to surface in Corona. The city began to experience rapid growth. The population for Riverside County in 1960 was 306,191.

Some old-time residents have vivid memories of being young in Corona in the 1960s. There were rumors of haunting tales of ghosts encountered in the orchards or seen around the old mansions. One was a skeleton of a grove worker that would come out at night, whistling as he clacked along. Another dealt with the ghost of pilots who had crashed in the hills above Corona, seeking a way home through the lemon and orange groves.

In 1962, the Citizens Advisory Committee was formed to advise the city council and airport manager. In 1964, Stanford Research Institute's study urged the expansion of the Corona Airport because of the expected growth in the area. The study also recommended many improvements to other airports in Riverside County. In 1967, there was a flood brought on by rain.

In 1969, the Corona Airport was completely rebuilt, and a 3,200-foot runway was constructed on its present location. In 1972, Joe Greer, retired Corona police chief, became the part-time airport manager. He held that position until 1989.

In 1972, tract homes and the Meadowview Country Club were built northwest of Corona Airport. In 1977, consultants were hired to plan possible improvement and expansion of the airport, including adding a second runway. In 1979, the FAA suggested a tower and a full-time manager for Corona Airport. At the time, there were an estimated five hundred planes based there.

In February 1980, the airport flooded again due to heavy rains. Also in 1980, the first phase was completed of the $303,870 flood improvement project using state grant funds. The airport was also seeking an additional grant of $242,000 to install a complete drainage system.

In 1983, there was an estimated 128,480 operations, not including touch-and-goes. A year later, that number increased to 132,860 operations, not including touch-and-goes.

In 1985, homes were built on the southwest corner of Lincoln and River Road, a short distance from the airport. In 1986, the Bell's Vireos bird was declared endangered. There were thirty known pairs of the birds in the Prado Basin.

In 1987, the operations of the airport (not including touch-and-goes) increased again to 137,970. Also in 1987, the Norco Rotary Club, spearheaded by Joe Nugent, developed a plan to take advantage of the resources at the Corona Municipal Airport in the event of a major disaster, such as an earthquake. The resources included at least five hundred airplanes and helicopters, water, fuel supplies, communications radios and shelter. More than one hundred pilots volunteered to survey the area for damage from the air or transport the injured or paramedics. The airport would provide landing space for planes and helicopters coming into the area to help. In 1987, pilots used a new approach for landing at Corona Airport. Pilots started using "dog-leg," or a slightly curved approach, which followed the dry wash and then jogged over to line up straight with the runway.

In 1988, Meadowlark Airport in Huntington Beach, California, was closed, and many of the planes from there were relocated to Corona Airport.

In 1989, Lewis Hull became the interim airport manager, replacing Joe Greer. There was an airport study conducted, and a count of the number of takeoffs and landings was done to determine if a control tower was merited. The FAA discussed the possibility with the Corona Airport Advisory Committee. It was determined that there would need to be a minimum of 200,000 takeoffs and landings per year to warrant a tower. In March 1989, work began on an improvement project that was approved in October 1988 and cost more than $600,000. Work included a sewer system and an architect for new administration and restaurant buildings. The Army Corps of Engineers approved the sewer system. A new automated weather-reporting station was installed at no cost to the city. In April 1989, Richard Paradee resigned from the Corona Airport Advisory Committee. The seat was filled by a city council member. In addition, Daniel A. Whitfield was appointed to replace Robert W. Whitfield.

In 1990, an environmental impact study was conducted. In January 1993, Ken Calvert resigned from the Airport Advisory Committee in order to take his office as the newly elected congressman. In February 1993, the airport was again flooded due to heavy rains. In September 1993, airport manager Brian Raber presented the Corona Municipal Airport Flood Evacuation Plan to the city council.

In September 1994, the airport held the Wings and Wheels event for the community. In May 1995, the Corona Municipal Airport Commission was formed. In September 1996, Wings and Wheels was once again held for the

In approximately 1925, there was a flying field located at the Parkridge Country Club northeast of Corona. Corona Airport is on land leased by the Army Corps of Engineers in the vicinity of Prado Dam. *Courtesy City of Corona.*

community. This was an annual event for several years. In 1997, the Corona Municipal Airport flood control protection plan and negative declaration Phase One was put into action. This phase included flood walls to both the north and south. Phase Two included improvements to outlet drains.

In January 1998, John Elwell was appointed interim airport manager. In February of that year, the airport was again subject to floodwaters. In June 1998, the FAA turned down a request for a control tower that was promoted by the chamber of commerce. The reason was that the city did not qualify for funding under FAA guidelines. In October 1998, Bill Cobb was named airport manager.

In 1999, the number of Bell's Vireos increased to an estimated two hundred pairs in the Prado Basin.

In August 2000, the Army Corps of Engineers began construction of a new dike upstream of the Prado Dam. In February 2001, an oil-water separator (clarifier) was installed on aircraft wash racks. In April of the same year, a police satellite station opened at the airport manager's office. In September 2001, 2002, 2003, 2004 and 2005, the airport held an annual community event called Airfaire.

Richard Brodeur became the manager of Corona Airport in 2004, following a line of airport managers that started with Joe Greer in 1947. Greer was then a police captain with the Corona Police Aero Squadron. He was named part-time airport manager in 1972 and held the position until he retired in 1989. *Courtesy City of Corona.*

In May 2004, Richard Brodeur was named airport manager. In March 2005, the airport was yet again subject to heavy flooding. Also this year, the DC3 Rose was filmed for the World War II docudrama *Miriam*.

The Corona Municipal Airport has been called the "Friendliest Little Airport in America" by those who have flown into the facility.

Representatives from the California Aeronautic Commission favored a site owned by the federal government in the Prado Basin. The City Airport Committee was instrumental in the early years of the airport's relocation.

The Army Corps of Engineers leases the airport land to the City of Corona on a month-to-month basis for a nominal fee per year. The city has the responsibility for developing and operating the airport. The airport is on one hundred acres with an east–west runway. The land is located in a flood

Corona Airport is located in a flood area and has been subjected to major floods every ten years. *Courtesy City of Corona.*

plain and has been subjected to major floods every ten years (and two floods in the last eight years).

The airport has 276 hangars, an estimated 453 pilots and a number of smaller businesses on the property. The airport is home to 350 to 400 general aviation aircraft with no commercial flights. The small airport is extremely active, with approximately fifty thousand annual operations. The airport has earned the California Aid to Airports Program Grant (CAAP) from the California Department of Transportation to assist with the operations of the facility.

Pilots who have flown from or to Corona Airport include retired generals, Jet Propulsion Laboratory (JPL) employees, pilots flying biplanes and experimental aircraft and a handful of Hollywood celebrities. In the early days, Steve McQueen and John Travolta flew into Corona Airport, and in more recent times actor Harrison Ford landed at Corona.

For thirty-six years, Bob and Meta Suko owned and operated the café at the Corona Airport known as Bob's Chili and Chow Hall. They opened the restaurant in 1974 and witnessed many changes to the facility over the years.

In recent years, the airport has held public events to gain public awareness of the facility. For the past two years, each June, the facility has

For thirty-six years, Bob and Meta Suko owned and operated the café at Corona Airport known as Bob's Chili and Chow Hall. They opened the café in 1974 and witnessed many changes to the area and the airport over the years. *Author's photo.*

In recent years, the airport has held public events to gain community awareness of the facility. *Courtesy City of Corona.*

For the past two years in June, the airport has held the Mud Run. Participants ranged in age from very young to seniors. *Courtesy City of Corona.*

held the Mud Run. An estimated three thousand participants maneuvered through an obstacle course in the mud. All ages participated, from young to seniors. An estimated six thousand on-lookers cheered for the muddy participants.

FLABOB AIRPORT

FAA Identifier:	RIR
Lat./Long.:	33-59-19.6000N / 117-24-35.9000W 33-59.326667N / 117-24.598333W 33.9887778 / -117.4099722 (estimated)
Elevation:	764 ft. / 233 m. (estimated)
Variation:	13E (2010)
From City:	3 miles NW of central business district of the associated city
Time Zone:	UTC -8 (UTC -7 during Daylight Saving Time)
Zip Code:	92509

Flabob is the fifth-oldest surviving civil airport in California and the seventh-oldest surviving airport of any kind in California.

Several individuals were responsible for creating and fostering the airfield, among them Roman Warren, Flavio Madariaga and Bob Bogen ("Flabob" being the combination of the first names of the latter two men), as well as Tom Wathen, who had the ability and wisdom to move the airfield into the twenty-first century and still keep the charm and romance of the 1930s and '40s. Flabob is known as the "Little Airport that Time Forgot."

"The Little Airport that Time Forgot." Flabob Airport is the seventh-oldest surviving airport in California, founded in 1925 as Riverside's first civil airport. *Courtesy of Tom Wathen Center.*

Front of Flabob Airport. *Courtesy of John D. Lyon.*

Roman Warren, nicknamed the Cowboy Aviator. Riverside Airport, 1936. *Courtesy of Roman Warren Jr. and family.*

In recent years, the facility has blossomed with new life. Located approximately fifty miles from Los Angeles, Flabob has had a colorful history. In the 1920s, Roman Warren, known as the Cowboy Aviator, put the airport on the map and contributed to its early history.

Roman Warren

In his book *Cowboy Aviator*, noted Riverside historian Robert J. Fitch masterfully describes Roman Warren's activities in early Riverside. Roman Warren was a skilled horseman and airplane pilot. In 1923, he was flying his plane to Los Angeles to be part of a movie when he ran out of gas in Riverside. He was forced to land his plane just west of Mount Rubidoux and the Santa Ana River. That turn of events helped bring Riverside into the age of aviation. It was at this landing that he met Johnny Hammond, who would grow to become a lifelong friend to Warren. (Warren taught Hammond how to fly.) Warren decided to establish an airport. Arthur M. Sweet, who owned a clothing store in downtown Riverside, helped him in his quest. In 1918, Sweet had worked with Frank Miller from the Mission Inn to help create March Field.

Roman Warren was born in Joliet, Illinois, in 1893. He was one of eight children raised by a single mother. He left home when he was ten to work as a driver for a horse and carriage. When he was fourteen, he went to Kansas and rode the rails. He worked by stocking coal and other duties to help out the railroad men. He next went on to Montana to become a cowboy. He learned how to rope and ride and do the other jobs of the ranch. His standard pay for the summer months was thirty dollars a month. In the winter months, he took other jobs like stagecoach driver and deputy sheriff.

Warren was in Chicago during World War I. While he was there, he got acquainted with some pilots who were flying in the war. One of the men took Warren into the sky in a Curtis JN4D Jenny. He got his first taste of flying. After the war, Roman Warren bought a war surplus plane in a crate for a few hundred dollars. He assembled it and began flying. His next adventure was being a barnstormer. Barnstorming was the first major form of civil aviation in the history of flight. The typical fee for a ride with a barnstormer was five dollars. Barnstormers were traveling gypsies who moved from town to town. Planes were not sophisticated or complicated; they had only air speed indicators, altimeters and gas gauges. He started the Roman Warren Flying Circus, bringing thrills and adventure from town to town.

In 1925, Roman Warren first performed at the Southern California Fair, held in Riverside in October. The Southern California Fair took place each October between 1915 and 1930. Warren did aerial acrobatics: stunts, rolls and dives with his plane, and when he was finished, he put on his cowboy hat and got out of the plane in full cowboy attire. He went from the cockpit to his horse, Monty, and galloped to the grandstands. It was easy to see how he gained fame as the "Cowboy Aviator."

Barnstorming had begun to decline by the mid-1920s. Federal regulations required pilots to have licenses, as set forth in the Air Commerce Act of 1926.

Purple Sash Rancho

In 1926, Roman Warren established a ranch, cabin and riding club near the Santa Ana River. He called his ranch the Purple Sash Rancho. The members of the club wore purple sashes, hence the name. He started it to provide an opportunity for outdoor fun and exercise for young men and women. The fee for membership was two dollars, and monthly dues were one dollar. In 1927, a movie was filmed near the rancho about American Indians. Warren's actions and friendliness caused the Indians to hold a ceremony and welcome him into the Sioux tribe. He was named "Flying Horse."

Ethel Berry Warren

In 1927, Roman Warren married Ethel Berry dressed in full western attire, complete with chaps and cowboy hats. Ethel was an excellent horsewoman and was skilled as a trick rider. She and Roman performed together in rodeos and horse shows. Roman taught Ethel how to fly a plane, and it wasn't long before she was able to solo. Ethel died in 1997 at the age of eighty-eight.

Celebrities

During the 1920s and '30s, many celebrities had the opportunity to fly with or visit Roman Warren. Some of these included baseball great Babe Ruth and movie stars Bebe Daniels and Jack Pickford, the brother of film legend Mary Pickford. Cowboy movie star Ken Maynard stopped by the airport to visit with Roman. Pilots flying from March Field often landed at Roman Warren's airport.

Roman's First Flight Under a Bridge

Early in 1919, Roman bought a surplus Jenny in a crate, assembled it and headed out to live the life of a barnstormer. He flew from town to town, doing loop-the-loops and whifferdills, substituting for the parachutist when the latter was too drunk to jump and having many adventures. In Peoria, he buzzed a bridge to see the people on it scatter, but the engine in his Nieuport quit, and he had no choice but to fly under the bridge. Once under it, he dragged the tail in the water and "pancaked" onto the shore.

Barnstorming had lost its charm by the mid-'20s, as the field became crowded, the crowds became jaded and the dollars became scarce. Roman remembered Riverside, where he had dead-sticked a landing on a vacant field at Indiana and Chicago Streets, having run out of gas on his way to Los Angeles.

In 1924, Roman returned and helped to run a field on Jurupa Avenue. In 1925, the City of Riverside created a Commission on Aeronautics, took control of the Mission Boulevard field and had it cleared of brush by the Junior Lions Club. Warren flew from the Jurupa field and made the first landing in a Jenny, avoiding the stumps and brush, which were still present. The lessor, Pliny Evans, had retained the right of pasturage, and

Roman Warren and two unidentified people in a barnstorming flight in 1925. Barnstorming had lost its charm by the mid-'20s. Roman remembered Riverside, where he had dead-sticked a landing on a vacant field at Indiana and Chicago Streets, having run out of gas on his way to Los Angeles. A school boy, Johnny Hammond, helped him find a place to stay and the next day got tickets printed for barnstorming rides. In 1924, Roman returned and helped to run a field on Jurupa Avenue. *Courtesy of Roman Warren Jr. and family.*

Roman's first job was to build a barbed-wire corral, not for the cows, but to put the airplanes in at night so the cows did not eat the sweet doped fabric covering.

Business was not good. An airport in 1925 was not much like one of the twenty-first century. No one went to the airport to catch a plane to somewhere; only a few hundred passengers flew in 1925, perched on top of the mail sacks in open-cockpit biplanes. It was a year before the Air Commerce Act, which first brought the national government into civil aeronautics. It was two years before Lindbergh flew the Atlantic solo and brought about the "Lindbergh boom" in aviation. Warren could make a living only by teaching students to fly, giving "joyrides" to air-minded citizens, flying an occasional charter or package delivery and, on rare occasions, selling gas or hangar storage to transient pilots.

Seeking to increase his business by publicity, he remembered his inadvertent flight under the bridge in Peoria and announced that he would fly under the Rubidoux bridge over the Santa Ana River, only a few hundred feet from his "Riverside Airport."

Roman Warren on a horse at the beginning of Riverside Airport, later known as Flabob. *Courtesy of Roman Warren Jr. and family.*

In 1938, Roman Warren arranged with the post office to transport the mail from Indio to Glendale with stops in Palm Springs, Banning and Riverside. It was a history-making event, and Warren autographed many first-day issues at the Riverside post office. *Courtesy of Roman Warren Jr. and family.*

In 1927, Roman Warren re-created his famous flight under the bridge at the Southern California Fair. *Courtesy of Roman Warren Jr. and family.*

In due course, as publicity spread, business did pick up, and Warren gave flying lessons to Riverside mayor Joseph S. Long and a number of businessmen, lawyers and doctors. He had flown in the first Southern California Fair and Fiesta de Anza in 1925, flying the Thomas-Morse against a racing automobile driven by Riverside's hometown-favorite race driver, Johnny Vicker.

Roman's Re-created Flight Under a Bridge

In 1927, Roman was asked to repeat his bridge flight under a specially constructed wooden arch in front of the grandstand. The arch opening was the same as that of the Rubidoux bridge, but a little narrower. Warren made the flight thirteen times during the 1927 and 1928 fairs but then quit because it seemed to him that the crowd was more hopeful for a gory crash than appreciative of precision flying.

Perhaps the bridge flight publicity did some good because three months later, on September 17, 1926, Warren was hired to fly oilman Edwin Pauley and his district manager, Helmer Duncan, to the opening of a

In 1926, Roman Warren was seeking to increase his business by publicity when he remembered his inadvertent flight under a bridge in Peoria and announced that he would fly under the Rubidoux bridge over the Santa Ana River, only a few hundred feet from his "Riverside Airport." *Courtesy of Roman Warren Jr. and family.*

new gas station in El Centro. Pauley's Eureka Oil Company furnished the lubricating oil for Warren's ships and had its name painted on the lower wings. Warren flew the pair to El Centro in a Bird cabin biplane, with two passengers inside and the pilot outside. The next day, on takeoff for the return trip, the ninety-horsepower OX-5 suffered a partial power loss, and the ship clipped a high-tension line and dove in nose-first. Warren was trapped, dangling upside down from a flying wire. He had a pair of pliers in his pocket and was able to pull the cotter pin out of the wire terminal and drop to the ground. He pulled Pauley and Duncan out of the fuselage and crawled to a farmhouse for help. Duncan was killed, and Pauley's neck was broken, but he survived, bedridden for a year. Had Pauley died, history might have been very different, because he went on to become the treasurer of the Democratic Central Committee and, more than anyone else, was responsible for Harry S Truman's nomination as vice president in 1944.

Roman Warren had flown the refueling ship for the successful women's endurance flight of Bobbi Trout and Elinor Smith at Metropolitan Airport in Van Nuys, California. Roman had a variety of jobs to make ends meet, and at this time, in addition to running Riverside Airport, he was chief pilot for the Commercial Airplane Company of Los Angeles, which made the Sunbeam in which Trout and Smith set their record.

Airport Improvements

In a 1927 issue of *Aviation* magazine, J.S. Hammond recounted the improvements at the airport: "The airport has been re-graded, lengthened, and leveled. Anything from a little flivver to an all-metal transport has landed on this field. Like any good airport a general invitation is extended to any and all pilots to make use of the field when flying cross-country." Riverside Airport was incorporated on July 11, 1927, with Roman Warren named as president, C. Lisle Stalder as vice-president and C.W. Bill Seaton as secretary-treasurer. Warren's friend Johnny Hammond was named field manager. Gasoline pumps were added, and a black-and-white windsock was placed on the hangar roof. Warren also added a large airport sign located at the end of the field. The Riverside Realty Board collected money for the creation of the sign.

On July 4, 1930, the four Hunter brothers (Albert, Kenneth, John and Walter) landed in Chicago after setting a new endurance record of 553 hours, 41 minutes, 30 seconds in the air—more than three weeks aloft. The endurance airplane and the refueling airplane were both Stinson Detroiters SM-1Bs: NR5189, the City of Chicago, and NR5326, Big Ben. They landed in Riverside to refuel on their way to Hollywood.

In September 1932, an air show was held at Riverside Airport during California Aviation Week. The *Riverside Daily Press* reported that approximately five thousand people attended. Events included parachute jumps, aerobatics, radio-controlled airplane maneuvers, demonstrations and Roman Warren flying the airmail letters that were postmarked at the airport by the postmaster. During California Aviation Week, a model airplane show was held at March Field.

On August 12, 1918, the Post Office Department took over airmail service from the U.S. Army Air Service (USAAS). Assistant postmaster general Otto Praeger appointed Benjamin B. Lipsner, who left the USAAS, to head the civilian-operated Airmail Service. In 1938, Roman Warren

A P-12 approaching Flabob Airport in 1935. *Courtesy of Roman Warren Jr. and family.*

Flabob Airport in the 1940s. *Courtesy of Tom Wathen Center.*

began flying the mail for Riverside. He did this at his own expense. He arranged with the post office to fly the mail from Indio to Glendale. He made stops in Palm Springs, Banning and Riverside. This was a history-making event pioneering airmail in the Riverside area. In commemoration of the event's first day, cachets were printed, and Warren autographed over 2,500 of these first-day issues.

During World War II, Warren spent his time as a civilian instructor training pilots for the United States Army Air Corps. At the time, since he was too old for active duty in the war, he gained the nickname "Pop" from many of his students. Roman Warren died on August 19, 1991. Roman and Ethel are buried at Olivewood Cemetery in Riverside, California. He will long be remembered for the aviation contributions that he made to Riverside.

After the original Riverside Airport was washed away in the flood of 1938, the few pilots who stayed on moved their airplanes a few hundred yards downstream, where a leftover Works Progress Administration (WPA) toolshed provided some shelter and is now incorporated into Flabob's Hangar One. When World War II started, a Civil Air Patrol Squadron was established at the airport.

In 1943, the little airstrip was bought by Flavio Madariaga and his partner, Bob Bogen.

Flavio Madariaga

Madariaga was a jack-of-all-trades—a pilot and a machinist who could make anything. He and his partner, Bob Bogen, an aeronautical engineer, owned a machine shop in Los Angeles. Foreseeing the difficulty of continuing this kind of business in Los Angeles as population and land values soared, Madariaga and Bogen looked for a place farther out, with room for an airstrip to enable them to make aerial delivery of supplies and parts and to bring in customers. They drew a fifty-mile circle from Los Angeles City Hall and looked at a number of possible places. According to Flabob legend, they rejected many possible strips as too scenic and therefore likely to become densely settled. They settled on the little airstrip adjoining the village of Rubidoux, close to the city of Riverside. Madariaga moved there with his family. He had done a lot of work for the movie studios, such as making the "vines" on which Tarzan swung, and he scrounged a circus tent from one of the studios, which was pitched under a tree and became the family home. For a while, meals were on a picnic table under the tree, and the still-roaming cows helped themselves to any tasty bits they found on the table. The tent is long gone, but the tree is still there and so were the cows, until a developer ran them off a couple years ago.

Bob Bogen in the early 1940s. Flavio Madariaga and Bob Bogen combined the first letters of their first names to come up with "Flabob." In the earliest directories, it was "Fla Bob," then it became "Fla-Bob" and then "FlaBob." Today, the airport is known throughout the world simply as "Flabob." *Courtesy of Don Madariaga.*

Madariaga was a world-class scrounger who could make or build just about anything, and Flabob Airport is literally the product of his mind and hands. He was quick to take advantage of opportunities when they were offered. After the war, he bought a surplus trainer and was flying it back to Flabob over the desert area where General Patton had trained his tank corps. He saw a group of men near stacks of wood and landed to inquire. He learned that the men had bought the crates in which Patton's tanks had been delivered as surplus. The crates had been made of one-inch oak and were, to Madariaga's mind, just what he needed to build sturdy hangars at the airport. All his money had been spent on the plane, so he offered it to the crate owners if they would deliver the wood to the airport. The men said that, not knowing how to fly, they had no use for an airplane, but the resourceful Madariaga threw in flying lessons, and the deal was done. The huge pile of wood gradually became hangars and structures at the airport. The wood was so hard that it was necessary to drill holes in it to start the nails.

Flavio hauled one hundred tons of oak back to Flabob. He also transported two thousand feet of used two-inch pipe for hangar construction. Flavio

Flavio Madariaga and his business partner, Bob Bogen, purchased a dirt airstrip nestled between the small town of Rubidoux and the city of Riverside in Southern California. It was Madariaga's personality and talent that shaped the airport. For forty years, he built it up, often with his own hands, making it a haven for people who are passionate about building and flying airplanes. *Courtesy of Don Madariaga.*

even built his house out of surplus materials. In an interview in *AOPA Pilot* magazine, he commented, "You've gotta be a sort of horse trader to make a private airport pay off." A lot of private airports usually start as small family-owned operations.

Other buildings came from surplus at March Field. Madariaga explained that his donkey, Napoleon, and some chickens borrowed from the neighbors made him a "farmer" and thus eligible for such surplus structures. The airport was still called simply "Riverside Airport" until emergency crews responding to a crash at Riverside Arlington Airport came to it by mistake. After that incident, the airport was renamed Flabob.

"When you come into my airport, you line up with the cross, close the throttle, bless yourself, turn left and land," said Flavio Madariaga.

Leading up to and during World War II, many United States military bases experienced growth in support of the war effort, but as the war

Dedication of Flabob Airport on September 30, 1949. *Courtesy of Don Madariaga.*

came to a close, much of this expansion was no longer needed. This created a market of war surplus items, as in the case of U.S. Army Camp Hahn. In 1946, Camp Hahn, adjacent to March Field (which is now March Air Reserve Base), became part of March Field, and its structures began to be sold off as war surplus. Flavio Madariaga saw this as a great opportunity and tried to buy some of the buildings. However, Flavio was quick to learn that the government imposed an eligibility requirement that the surplus buildings were to be sold only to farmers and clergymen. With the purchase of a wagon, a donkey and some chickens, along with his horse and dog, Flavio had a photograph taken of himself, which he then used to qualify himself as a farmer. This made him eligible to bid on some of the surplus buildings, which he did successfully, and had them moved to Flabob.

In 1949, one of these surplus buildings, which is said to have been the cookhouse for the Noncommissioned Officers' Club (NCO), became and still is the home to the Flabob Airport Café, a place well known in the aviation community that unofficially serves as Flabob Airport's historical society and museum of sorts. This surplus building was a vast

After the original Riverside Airport was washed away in the flood of 1938, the few pilots who stayed on moved their airplanes a few hundred yards downstream, where a leftover WPA toolshed provided some shelter and is now incorporated into Flabob's Hangar One. With World War II looming, a Civil Air Patrol Squadron was established there. In 1943, the little strip was bought by Flavio Madariaga and his partner, Bob Bogen. *Courtesy of Don Madariaga.*

It usually takes the fun out of a joke to explain it, but you who are much younger may not know that the adjective "one-horse" is old-timey slang for "really small," as in "one-horse town." *Courtesy of Tom Wathen Center.*

The late famed aviation cartoonist Bob Stevens saw the photo, and it inspired this cartoon. *Courtesy of Tom Wathen Center.*

improvement over the lean-to that was constructed on the side of Hangar One, which was itself a tatted-up WPA tool and equipment shed left over from the New Deal. Many aircraft designs and improvements first saw the light as sketches on napkins at the café. The café's walls are filled to capacity with old photos, memorabilia and airplane junk, with big model airplanes hovering overhead.

Flavio was quick to take advantage of opportunities when they were offered. Here is one example: In Riverside, on Magnolia near Arlington, where the streetcar line ran, was the Bluebonnet Drive-In. It was closed, but Flavio was on the alert, and he bought the building and moved it over to Flabob. He removed the spaceship on the roof (actually, a support for floodlights), the neon sign and the awning. Some of the windows were filled

Flavio standing on the left of a plane. *Courtesy of John D. Lyon.*

in. The building was grafted onto Hangar Six, making it a "lean-to" in airport talk.

In 1962, Flavio established a business to fly lighted messages on planes at night. He called his business the "Fly by Night Sign Company." He outfitted his plane to carry ten five-foot-high neon letters under the wings of the plane. He even patented the design that changed the neon letters from a plastic disk. He supplied power for the sign from the generators of the airplane. He used two 110-volt inverters and then two 1,000-volt transformers.

Aviation Greats at Home at Flabob

For reasons unknown, Flabob Airport became synonymous with aviation greats and was home to aviators such as Margaret Ritchie, Frank Tallman and Art Scholl. Well-known aircraft designers such as Ed Marquart, Lou Stolp and Ray Stits also called Flabob home. But after the deaths of Bogen and Madariaga, keeping the doors of Flabob open started to become challenging. With the uncertainty that Flabob would continue to operate, many pilots moved on to greener pastures.

View of the hangars at Flabob Airport in the 1940s. *Courtesy of Tom Wathen Center.*

Frank Tallman

Frank was a Hollywood stunt pilot in the 1960s and '70s. He maintained a hangar at Flabob, which he used for restoring military aircraft. Tallman flew stunt planes in many notable movies, including *It's a Mad, Mad, Mad, Mad World* (he was the pilot who flew through the billboard), *The Carpetbaggers* (1964), *The Wrecking Crew* and *The Thousand Plane Raid.* Tallman also was the aerial coordinator and pilot for *Baa Baa Black Sheep* and flew in *Amelia Earhart,* both television projects in 1976.

Art Scholl

Art was one of the greatest aerobatic performers of all time. He owned and operated an aerobatic school and maintenance facility at Flabob for a number of years. Scholl was also a movie stunt pilot with more than two hundred commercials, television shows and films, including *The Right Stuff, The Great Waldo Pepper, Blue Thunder, A Team, CHIPS* and *Top Gun,* to his credit. After the Flabob Café moved to its new digs in 1949, the original lean-to became Art Scholl's apartment.

Bill Turner

Bill was a World War II Consolidated PBY Catalina pilot. After leaving the navy, Bill started Repeat Aircraft at Flabob. Over the years, Bill Turner and

Repeat Aircraft have built a number of replica aircraft, including the Miss Los Angeles, which was a replica of a 1934 air racer. He also built a replica of the Turner-Laird LTR-14 that Roscoe Turner used to win the Thompson Trophy in 1938–39, as well as several replica Gee Bees, a de Havilland Comet DH.88, the Miles and Attwood Special (which was the most winning racer during the big Cleveland air race years) and several other aircraft.

Lou Stolp

The legendary Lou Stolp designed and refined many aircraft, including the Starduster Too, AcroDuster Too, Starlet, V-Star, Super Starduster and Starduster One right at Flabob. The design rights to the popular Stolp Starduster line of home-built aircraft have been acquired by Aircraft Spruce & Specialty, where aircraft aficionados can purchase the plans and material kits necessary to construct one of these home-builts.

Margaret Ritchie

A natural pilot, Margaret's acrobatic abilities combined with the agility of the Akro won her the national women's aerobatics title in 1966.

Margaret Ritchie's acrobatic abilities combined with the agility of the Akro won her the national women's aerobatics title in 1966. Margaret flew and trained out of Flabob. *Courtesy of John D. Lyon.*

Margaret flew and trained out of Flabob, where her husband, George, and his partner, Clayton Stephens, refurbished and resold airplanes. Together they designed and built the acrobatic Akro for Margaret, which included a canopy design that would accommodate her beehive hairdo. Sadly, Margaret was killed in 1969 while flying her Akro, and as a symbol of her love for aerobatics, the Akro was cut into pieces and buried with her.

Ed Marquart

Having heard about Flabob through the EAA, Ed Marquart joined the Flabob family of designers and builders in 1955. Originally, Ed went to work for Ray Stits, but after a couple years, he was busy building his own aircraft design, the Marquart MA-3 Maverick and later the Marquart MA-4 Lancer, and then went on to his greatest achievement, the Marquart MA-5 Charger, several hundred of which were sold. Ed spent many years building some very notable racer replicas with Bill Turner. Aside from his

An unidentified pilot standing at Flabob in front of a Stits Skybaby, one of the world's smallest airplanes. *Courtesy of John D. Lyon.*

experience and expertise as a plane builder and designer, Ed was an early supporter of the EAA and served as Chapter One president for several years. Ed was another one of the great pioneers of aviation who called Flabob home.

Flabob can boast to be the birthplace of one of the world's smallest planes. In 1952, longtime Flabob resident and aircraft designer/builder Ray Stits built the Stits Sky Baby (Stits SA-2A Sky Baby-N5K), which flew many times at Flabob. With its seven-foot, two-inch span, the Stits Sky Baby held the title of the world's smallest biplane from 1952 through 1984. Shortly after securing the record, Ray donated the Stits Sky Baby to the National Air and Space Museum, which has had it on long-term loan to the EAA AirVenture Museum since 1963.

Experimental Aircraft Association EAA

For years, Flabob was a lively bed of activity for the design, manufacture and flying of experimental aircraft. Flabob is the site of the first chapter of the Experimental Aircraft Association (EAA).

The first chapter gathering was held in 1953, when Ray Stits and a number of close friends and fellow homebuilding enthusiasts met at Flabob Airport. Today, there are nearly one thousand active local EAA and divisional chapters and squadrons all over the world carrying on the tradition of recreational aviation.

The EAA is a growing and diverse organization of members with a wide range of aviation interests and backgrounds. The EAA was founded in 1953 by a group of individuals in Milwaukee, Wisconsin, who were interested in building their own airplanes. Through the decades, the organization expanded its mission to include antiques, classics, war birds, aerobatic aircraft, ultra lights, helicopters and contemporary manufactured aircraft. EAA is located in Oshkosh, Wisconsin.

Young Eagles

EAA Chapter One at Flabob has a vibrant Young Eagles program where dedicated volunteers educate and fly fifty to one hundred new Young Eagles children per month at Flabob Airport. Children learn the basics of flight, take a preflight check of an airplane and then take to the sky and view the earth from a totally different perspective. The free EAA student membership is open to current and past Young Eagles, ages eight to nineteen. As an EAA student member, they are entitled to a free student membership in the Academy of Model Aeronautics (AMA). AMA membership can help students get involved in all forms of aircraft modeling, from R/C (radio-controlled) to free flight and control-line flying.

Tom Wathen

After the glory decades of the 1920s, '30s and '40s through '70s, and the death of Flavio Madariaga and his wife, Bert, in 1984, the airport was static until June 1, 2000, when Tom Wathen purchased the facility.

Flabob is now home to the Tom Wathen Center, a nonprofit 501(c)(3) corporation dedicated to education through aviation. Founder Tom Wathen believes that aviation is a powerful stimulus to learning, especially the vital STEM subjects: science, technology, engineering and mathematics.

The mission statement: The Tom Wathen Center uses the fascination of flight to inspire the love of learning for successful careers and satisfying lives.

In 1999, Tom Wathen retired as chairman of Pinkerton's, the international security and detective firm, and set out to fulfill his longtime plan to devote his time and resources to charitable activities.

Thomas Wathen was born on October 5, 1929, in Vincennes, Indiana. He got interested in aviation at an early age by working around an airport and becoming a Civil Air Patrol cadet. After graduating from college, he joined the air force.

With the help and advice of friends, he determined that his Wathen Foundation would be dedicated to aviation education and preservation. It quickly became apparent that the foundation needed a facility for its work, in effect a "campus" where teachers, volunteers, young people and others could get together.

Knowing that Flabob Airport had long been for sale, Wathen thought it might be a good site for the foundation's work. When the Wathen Foundation inquired early in 2000 if Flabob was still for sale, it was told that it was too late, as an offer to purchase the land for non-aviation development was far advanced. Fortunately, when the family

Flavio Madariaga and his wife, Bertha Ann (Bert). Flavio was a flight instructor, an FAA-designated flight examiner, a captain in the Civil Air Patrol and a friend to all the tenants and visitors fortunate enough to walk the dusty byways of Flabob. In 1984, Flavio and Bert were killed in an airplane accident at Flabob. Their son, Don Madariaga, immediately stepped forward to assume responsibility of managing Flabob. *Courtesy of Don Madariaga.*

owners realized that the Wathen Foundation was serious in its interest in purchasing and preserving Flabob, they gave their enthusiastic support and cooperation to the effort. On May 31, 2000, the Wathen Foundation completed its purchase of Flabob Airport.

Under the ownership of the Wathen Foundation and its airport arm, Flabob, LLC, many needed improvements have been made to Flabob Airport. The 3,200-foot runway has been widened and resurfaced, the parallel taxiway has been resurfaced and extended the entire length of the runway and aircraft parking areas and taxi lanes have been paved. The airport café has been refurnished, repainted and otherwise improved. Two new hangars have been built, and twelve more are nearing completion. Antiquers, restorers and builders will be especially welcome in these new hangars. A large new hangar and meeting place for EAA Chapter One

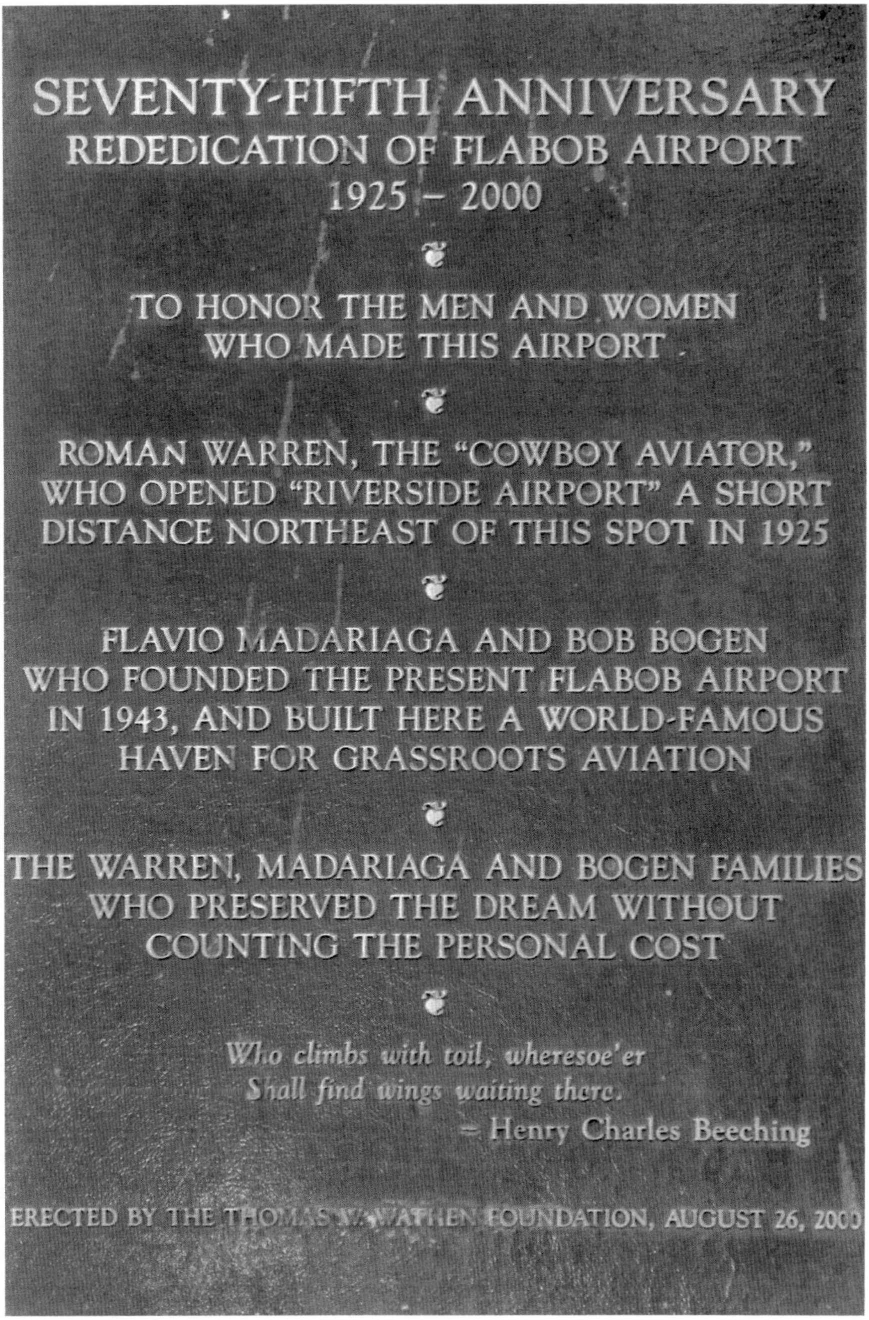

This plaque from 2000 commemorates the anniversary and rededication of Flabob.

was dedicated at Chapter One's fiftieth anniversary open house and will be a place for meetings and programs of many aviation organizations in addition to EAA Chapter One. Aviation-related businesses are welcome. Polyfiber, the world's leading manufacturer of aircraft fabric and coatings, is located at Flabob. Marquart Aviation remained at Flabob until Ed's passing. Several restorers, repair facilities, specialized fabricators and related businesses have recently gone into business at the field, and proposals from others have been solicited.

Under the direction of Dr. Art Peterson, president of the Wathen Academy, the educational programs at Flabob are a solid and growing community asset. The EAA Aviation Foundation worked with the Wathen Foundation to present the first of Oshkosh offerings of its Air Academy programs for young people, and these have now become a Flabob staple, with some four to six programs annually for middle and high school students. The programs each last several days and are designed not only to inform but also to motivate the students to work hard in school, especially in the areas of mathematics, science and technology.

Many parents have reported a remarkable increase in studiousness and even in civility after these programs. Wathen Academy personnel and volunteers also bring programs to area elementary, middle and high schools and leave a display of aviation magazines and publications, constantly refreshed, for the youngsters to read, take home and enjoy. Under foundation sponsorship, middle and high school students rebuilt a 1941 Aeronca Super Chief under expert adult supervision and earned subsidized flying lessons. Two follow-up projects are underway: a Stinson 108-3, donated by a group headed by EAA secretary Alan Shackleton, and a Stits Sky Coupe. A group recruited from an area youth gang learned aircraft covering under the expert tutelage of Polyfiber experts and has now formed its own business to offer aircraft recovering under continuing quality control from qualified experts. A public charter school, Flabob Airport Preparatory Academy, operates at the airport with support from the Wathen Foundation. Future expansion of aviation education at Flabob may take many forms but will continue to stress the value of such learning, not only for aviation itself but also as a powerful motivator for learning in many areas, for good citizenship and for leadership.

The airport includes all people, especially youth, veterans and the disadvantaged and challenged. At the historic Flabob Airport, there is excitement in working with the head, the hands and heart, side by side with pilots, craftsman and innovators in an authentic workplace. The airport

A twelve-foot replica of the Wright Flyer is mounted on a steel pylon near the entrance of Flabob. This was seen in 2003 in the Pasadena Tournament of Roses Parade. *Author's photo.*

preserves and disseminates the history of aviation and encourages and nourishes the designers, builders and innovators of tomorrow.

Each year, the Wathen Foundation conducts up to five five-day programs for middle and high school students, giving them a broad introduction to aviation science, including weather, navigation and the theory of flight. Programs include a number of hands-on activities and culminate in a Young Eagle airplane flight.

The Wathen Foundation offers introduction-to-aviation activities for fifth and sixth graders in this after-school program. Team members from the foundation visit the elementary schools for two sessions to share the theory and fundamentals of flight. The third session is a field trip to Flabob Airport, where participants are introduced to a variety of airplanes and hands-on experiences.

In these projects, small groups of young people, under close and expert adult supervision, rebuild airplanes and earn subsidized flying lessons. "We believe that restoration projects like this give high school students an opportunity to focus their interests and energies on positive life-enhancing

De Havilland Comet airplane. *Author's photo.*

Flabob Airport Preparatory Academy is a tuition-free, public charter high school and middle school (grades seven through twelve) located on Flabob Airport and operated by River Springs Charter School. It offers a broad liberal education, emphasizing science, mathematics, engineering and technology and using aviation as a context, example and motivator. *Courtesy of John D. Lyon.*

programs," said Tom Wathen. "In a sense, the airplane builds the kids, not the other way around."

The pilot training program is unique and highly prized by its students. It involves the subsidization of flight lessons for those students who have

The trustees of the Tom Wathen Center include Thomas W. Wathen, founding trustee and chairman; Jerry Barto, businessman and philanthropist; Arthur M. Butler, retired military and foundation director; Jon Goldenbaum, president of consolidated coatings; John D. Lyon, chairman of the board of trustees; Kevin J. McKenzie, attorney at law; and Richard D. Roth, attorney at law and major general (ret.), USAFR. *Courtesy of John D. Lyon.*

contributed significantly to the restoration of the project aircraft. The program has already produced twenty-four private pilots, many of whom have gone on to the nation's top undergraduate aviation programs, such as the University of North Dakota and Embry Riddle.

MARCH AIR FIELD

FAA Identifier:	RIV
Lat./Long.:	33-52-54.9870N / 117-15-32.4530W 33-52.916450N / 117-15.540883W 33.8819408 / -117.2590147 (estimated)
Elevation:	1536 ft. / 468 m. (estimated)
Variation:	14E (1980)
From City:	6 miles SE of RIVERSIDE, CA
Time Zone:	UTC -7 (UTC -8 during Standard Time)
Zip Code:	92518

March Air Reserve Base was originally known as Alessandro Field. The airfield was often used by pilots on flights to and from San Diego. Frank Miller was the owner of the famed Riverside Mission Inn at the time, and he and other prominent Californians contacted the War Department to gain approval for the construction of a military airfield in Riverside. Miller had acquired land that would be suitable to use as an airfield. In a document between Frank Miller and the United States of America, Miller gave the land to the U.S. government for a fee of $1 per month for the first five months. The document goes on to indicate the remaining terms of the gift: $64,000 for the purchase of 640 acres that was to be used for the airfield.

March Field main gate, 1928–early 1940s. *Author's photo.*

Due to the citrus boom, Riverside was a leading community in America at the time. A parade was held in Riverside to celebrate the future military airfield in February 1918. At the time, the United States was on the brink of entering World War I. Several European news sources reported significant German efforts to build a fleet of flying machines that could alter the nature of modern warfare and possibly carry the war to the skies. In response, Congress appropriated close to $640 million in early 1917 and attempted to back the plans of General George O. Squier, the army's chief signal officer. According to the California State Military Department, this move was an attempt "to put the Yankee punch into the war by building an army in the air." On March 20, 1918, Alessandro Flying Training Field became March Field in honor of Second Lieutenant Payton C. March Jr., son of the army chief of staff. He had enlisted in the United States Army on August 6, 1917, and was assigned to the Signal Corps Aviation Section. He trained in Toronto, Canada, and Austin, Texas.

On January 28, 1918, March was commissioned second lieutenant in the regular U.S. Air Corps after completing flying tests and gunnery instruction. Two weeks later, he was seriously injured in an airplane accident in San Antonio, Texas, and died in Fort Worth, Texas, on February 18, 1918. He

Modern building at March Field. *Courtesy of Danielle Bitetti.*

was buried at Arlington National Cemetery. The following month, on March 11, March Field, located ten miles southwest of Riverside, California, was named in his honor. It is now March Air Reserve Base.

Sergeant Charles E. Garlick was selected to help create the new military base. By April 1918, with the assistance of muleskinners from Colton, California, there was enough progress made that the first troops arrived. Captain William Carruthers served as the field's first commander.

Within sixty days, the land was transformed into twelve hangars, six barracks, mess halls, a machine shop, a post exchange, a hospital, a supply depot and aero repair building, bachelor officers' quarters and a residence for the commanding officer. After the end of the war in April 1923, March Field closed and remained quiet for a short period of time. In July 1926, Congress created the Army Air Corps, and funds were appropriated for the reopening of March Field, which took place in March 1927. Major Millard F. Harmon took over the job of base commander. Air force leaders such as Hoyt Vandenberg, Nathan Twining, Thomas Power and Curtis LeMay completed their initial flight training at March Field. Lieutenant Colonel Henry H. (Hap) Arnold was the base commander from 1931 to 1936.

U.S. Army consolidated PT-6A A.C. 30-385. *Author's photo.*

Arnold is called the "Father of the Modern Air Force." During the years he was in charge of the base, there was much development of the facility and the Army Air Corp on the base.

The lyrics and music to the "Army Air Corps Song," as it was originally known, or "The U.S. Air Force," as it is now known, were written by Captain Robert Crawford in 1939. In 1937, then second in command of the U.S. Army Air Corps Major General Arnold proposed a competition, with a prize for the winner, for a song reflecting the unique identity of the corps. About 757 compositions were entered and evaluated; no satisfactory songs were found. Just before the deadline, Crawford entered his song, which proved to be a unanimous winner. However, the U.S. Air Corps did not have enough money to widely publish the piece, so Crawford arranged a transfer of the song's copyright to a New York publisher, including a perpetual performance release in favor of the U.S. government. This means that, unlike other services, the USAF does not own its own service song.

Off we go into the wild blue yonder,
Climbing high into the sun;

Here they come zooming to meet our thunder.
At 'em boys, give 'er the gun!
Down we dive, spouting our flame from under,
Off with one hell of a roar!
We live in fame or go down in flame, Hey!
Nothing can stop the U.S. Air Force.

Over the years, many Hollywood celebrities such as Wallace Beery, Clark Gable, Red Skelton, Jimmy Durante, Desi Arnaz, Victor Borge, Harry James, George Burns, Gracie Allen, Groucho Marx, Bob Hope, Jack Benny and Joe E. Brown and famous aviators including Amelia Earhart visited March Field and brought much public awareness to the facility. Bob Hope made history by performing his radio show for a military audience. He performed his first USO (United Service Organizations) show at March in the gym in 1941. Hope was born in 1903 and died on July 27, 2003. He was a popular comedian and actor who appeared in vaudeville, on Broadway and in radio, television and movies. He performed for enlisted military from 1941 through the 1970s. He died in 2003 at the age of one hundred.

In 1938, Clark Gable filmed a movie on location at March Field named *Test Pilot*. In the movie, a reckless test pilot named Jim Lane (who was played by Clark Gable) is forced to land on a Kansas farm in his aircraft, the Drake Bullet SEV-S2 NR70Y, a modified civilian racer

Captain Edward "Eddie" Rickenbacker, commanding officer, Ninety-fourth Pursuit Squadron, World War I. *Author's photo.*

version of the U.S. Army Air Corps P-35, where he meets Ann Barton, played by Myrna Loy. They spend the day together and fall in love. They eventually get married, but Ann does not understand the danger that her husband faces flying experimental planes. By the end of the movie, Jim realizes how his flying experimental planes has disturbed his wife, and he decides to quit that kind of flying. The movie found favor with the critics when it was released. It is now considered to be historically significant for the planes and flying of the time.

The attack on Pearl Harbor in December 1941 brought March Field back into the business of training aircrews. Throughout the war, many soon-to-be-famous bombardment groups performed their final training at March before embarking for duty in the Pacific. During World War II, the base doubled in area and gained approximately seventy-five thousand troops. During active involvement in World War II, Camp Haan was established down the road from March. Camp Haan was officially established on January 10, 1941. It was named after Major General William George Haan. After the bombing in Pearl Harbor, the camp grew rapidly. By October 1941, Camp Haan had 353 buildings and twenty-eight miles of roads. The camp supported eighty-five thousand troops at the height of activity. It was used for training anti-artillery units. The camp received troops from around the United States because it was the only artillery training facility on the West Coast. After World War II, Camp Haan was a final destination for the military before returning to civilian life. The total investment for the camp was close to $18 million. After the war, it was viewed as surplus. All buildings and supplies were sold. The land known as Camp Haan is today part of March Air Reserve Base and also the Riverside National Cemetery.

According to the California State Military Department and the California State Military Museum, known units at March Field during World War II included:

PRESENT ON DECEMBER 7, 1941
Hq and Hq Sq, 4th Air Force Base Command
Hq and Hq Sq, 14th Pursuit Group (Fighter)
48th Pursuit Squadron (Fighter)
49th Pursuit Squadron (Fighter)
50th Pursuit Squadron (Fighter)
Hq and Hq Sq, 51st Pursuit Group (Fighter)
16th Pursuit Squadron (Fighter)
25th Pursuit Squadron (Fighter)

26th Pursuit Squadron (Fighter)
Hq and Hq Sq, 64th Transport Group
18th Transport Squadron
4th Photographic Squadron (1st Photographic Group)
Tow Target Detachment
Hq and Hq Sq, 32nd Air Base Group
43rd Material Squadron
44th Material Squadron
31st Air Base Squadron
Air Force Band
Det, 1st Communications Squadron
Det, 1st Weather Squadron
3rd Chemical Company (Service) (Aviation) (less Dets)
808th Engineer Battalion (Aviation)
682nd Ordnance Company (Aviation) (Pursuit)
693rd Ordnance Company (Aviation) (Pursuit)
718th Ordnance Company (Aviation) (Air Base)
Company L, 30th Quartermaster Regiment (Truck)
Det, Company D, 89th Quartermaster Battalion (Lt Maint)
4th Quartermaster Company (Supply) (Aviation) (less Dets)
4th Aircraft Warning Company
405th Signal Company (Aviation)
433rd Signal Maintenance Company (Aviation)
318th Signal Company (Air Wing)
854th Signal Service Company (Aviation) (less Dets)
4th Signal Platoon (Air Base)
420th Army Air Forces Base Unit (Combat Crew Training Station-Heavy)

The first Women Air Force Service Pilots (WASPs) arrived at March Air Field in January 1944. The WASP predecessors, the Women's Flying Training Detachment (WFTD) and the Women's Auxiliary Ferrying Squadron (WAFS), organized separately in September 1942. They were the pioneering organizations of the civilian female pilots, employed to fly military aircraft under the direction of the United States Army Air Forces during World War II. The WFTD and WAFS were merged on August 5, 1943, to create the paramilitary WASP organization. The female pilots of the WASP ended up numbering 1,074, each freeing a male pilot for combat service and duties. They flew over sixty million miles in every type of military aircraft. WASP was granted veteran status in 1977 and given the

General James Harold "Jimmy" Doolittle is depicted in an oil painting at the museum. *Author's photo.*

Congressional Gold Medal in 2009. Twenty-five thousand women applied to join WASP, but only 1,830 were accepted and took the oath. Out of these, only 1,074 passed the training and joined.

In April 1943, the Women's Army Auxiliary Corps (WAAC) arrived at March Field. At first, the women were used only as office support staff, but by the end of the war many of the women were also maintaining combat-ready aircraft. After the war, March became a Tactical Air Command Base.

The main unit, the famed First Fighter Wing, brought the first jet aircraft, the F-80, to the base. This deviation from the traditional bombardment

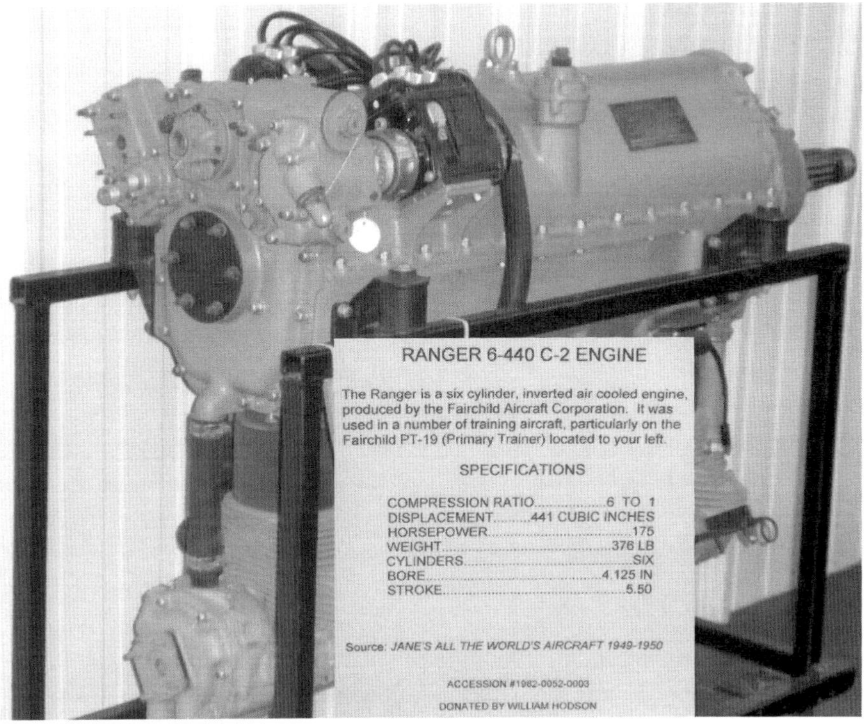

A Ranger 6-440 C-2 engine. The Ranger is a six-cylinder inverted air-cooled engine, produced by the Fairchild Aircraft Corporation. It was used in a number of training aircraft. *Author's photo.*

training and operations functions did not endure long. In 1949, March became part of the relatively new Strategic Air Command. Headquarters for the Fifteenth Air Force, along with the Thirty-third Communications Squadron, moved to March from Colorado Springs in the same year. Also in 1949, the Twenty-second Bombardment Wing moved from Smoky Hill Air Force Base, Kansas, to March. Thereafter, these three units remained dominant features of base activities. From 1949 to 1953, the B-29 Superfortresses dominated the flight line at March Air Force Base. For four months, July to October, the Twenty-second saw action over Korea. The wing converted from the propeller-driven B-29s to the B-47 jet bombers and their supporting tankers, the KC-97s. The KC-97s belonging to the Seventeenth and Twenty-second Air Refueling Squadrons represented a jump in technology.

In the spring of 1945, three armies converged on Germany. From the east, the Soviet forces were on the outskirts of Berlin, the capital of Nazi Germany. American and British forces were over one hundred miles west of it. Allied commander Dwight D. Eisenhower saw no point in racing toward the city simply to sacrifice lives to capture. Its fate was sealed, so he permitted it to be taken by the Soviet Union.

The Soviet armies occupied Poland, Czechoslovakia, Hungary, Bulgaria and the eastern half of Germany. France, Belgium and the Netherlands had been liberated by the Allies. Their forces occupied the western half of Germany. One result of this decision was the division of Germany into East and West, controlled by the Soviet Union and the Allies, respectively. Berlin was located in East Germany. The Allies divided the city into four sectors, each administered by a different country: Britain, France, the United States and the Soviet Union.

The Communist party ruled the Soviet Union. Its leader, Joseph Stalin, was a ruthless dictator. Under the Communist system, the government owned all property and tightly controlled the lives of citizens. The Allies were democracies that had popularly elected leaders. They were capitalistic. Property was owned by individuals and companies. The economy was characterized by free enterprise. Thus, there were two fundamentally different systems of government. World War II was far more devastating to the Soviets than to the Allies. Many of its cities were destroyed, and over twenty million people were killed.

On June 22, 1948, the Soviet Union imposed a blockade, cutting off all ground routes for the Allies to enter or leave Berlin. It was clearly an act of defiance and a test of Allied resolve. It seems as if the Allies would have no choice other than to evacuate the city. The Strategic Air Command (SAC) prepared for war. General Curtis LeMay was then commander of the U.S. Air Force, Europe. He saw the crisis as an opportunity to demonstrate American air power. He believed that the Allied forces could be supported by air. The Russians were surprised by the American resolve. By quickly asserting its force, the SAC blunted any thoughts the Soviets might have had of pushing their armies into Europe.

The B-29 Superfortress planes were in the forefront of the flight line at March Air Force Base from 1949 to 1953. The Twenty-second Bombardment Wing was involved in the Korean War in the early 1950s. After the Korean Conflict, the planes at March converted from the propeller B-29s to the B-47 jet bombers. It wasn't long before pilots and crews from March began setting new records in flying altitude and distance. The newer refueling planes presented global capabilities. In 1957, "Power Flight" general Archie Old led a flight of three B-52s in a nonstop around-the-world flight in a record forty-five hours and nineteen minutes. By the late 1960s, March Air Force Base had traded B47s and K-97s for sleek modern bombers and tankers.

For twenty years, the Twenty-second Bombardment Wing played a key role in the mission of the Strategic Air Command.

By the end of the 1960s, March Air Force Base was preparing to exchange its B-47s and KC-97s for updated bombers and tankers. By September 16, 1963, increasing international tensions in Europe and elsewhere brought March its first B-52B bomber, the City of Riverside. Soon, fifteen more bombers appeared on the flight line, along with new KC-135 jet Stratotankers. March's first KC-135, the Mission Bell, arrived on October 4, 1963. For the next twenty years, this new team would dominate the skies over what had come to be called the Inland Empire as the Twenty-second Bombardment Wing. It played a feature role in the Strategic Air Command's mission. During the conflict in Southeast Asia, the Twenty-second Bombardment Wing deployed its planes several times in operations such as Young Tiger, Rolling Thunder, Arc Light and Linebacker II. During the Vietnam era, the base served as a logistical springboard for supplies and equipment en route to the Pacific. Near the end of the conflict, March operated as one of the reception centers for returning prisoners of war. Following the end of hostilities in Southeast Asia, the Twenty-second returned to its duties as an integral part of the Strategic Air Command. For the next eighteen years, until 1982, March effectively supported America's defensive posture.

Several post-Vietnam adjustments brought the retirement of the wing's last B-52 on November 9, 1982. This event signaled yet another era for March Air Force Base and for the Twenty-second Bombardment Wing. After bombers were the key ingredient for so long, March became an air refueling wing with the new KC-10 tanker. The new tankers were able to accomplish considerably more than the KC-135s, and they promised a new tomorrow for the Strategic Air Command. Within months after the first KC-10 arrived at the base on August 11, 1982, crews quickly realized the ability of the new aircraft to carry cargo and passengers, as well as impressive fuel loads, over long distances. Air refueling for March Air Force Base had entered a new age. In 1982, the California Air National Guard came to March, bringing the F-4Cs.

Beginning in the early 1980s, the KC-10 became the vehicle carrying March Air Force Base into a new technological epoch. The large KC-10s, with their versatility and dependability, again gave the base a featured part in America's efforts to retain a strong and flexible military air arm. The utter importance of the KC-10s in conventional operations became particularly

This trainer plane is part of the splendid collection at March Field Air Museum. *Author's photo.*

apparent during Desert Shield and Desert Storm, where their outstanding service contributed measurably to the success of American forces in the defense of Saudi Arabia and the liberation of Kuwait.

In 1993, March Air Force Base was selected for realignment. In August 1993, the 445th Military Airlift Wing transferred to March from Norton Air Force Base in California. On January 3, 1994, the 22nd Air Refueling Wing was transferred to McConnell Air Force Base in Kansas, and the 722nd Air Refueling Wing stood up at March. As part of the U.S. Air Force's realignment and transition, March's two reserve units, the 445th Military Airlift Wing and the 452nd Air Refueling Wing, were deactivated, and their personnel and equipment were joined under the 452nd Air Mobility Wing on April 1, 1994. On April 1, 1996, March officially became March Air Reserve Base. For the over seventy years since March evolved from the dirt Alessandro Flying Strip, it has played a key role in the Inland Empire and in the advancement of aviation.

Colonel Glenn Tanner, commander of the 722nd Air Refueling Wing, March Air Force Base, prior to its realignment on April 1, 1996, to the 452nd

Air Mobility Wing, Air Force Reserve, holds the unique distinction of being the only non-rated wing commander of an air refueling wing that had no aircraft. They had all flown away!

The U.S. Air Force spent \$37 million in 1996 on remediation and was authorized to spend \$23 million in 1997. The initial cost estimate to restore March was set at about \$300 million and was to be completed by the year 2010. A fast-track cleanup initiative was expected to cost about \$170 million and was projected to be finished by 2000.

The 452nd Air Mobility Wing represents the only unit-equipped mobility wing in the reserves. The wing's KC-135 Stratotankers and C-141 Starlifters enable it to effectively perform a worldwide mission 365 days a year. It is the only air mobility wing in the U.S. Air Force Reserve Command that possesses all of the elements of an air mobility wing. The 163rd Air Refueling Wing (ANG) is a tenant unit at March Air Reserve Base that is assigned to the Air Mobility Command and the California Air National Guard.

The Fourth Air Force, part of the U.S. Air Force Reserve Command, is headquartered at March Air Force Base. The U.S. Air Force Reserve Command provides trained units and individuals to accomplish assigned duties in support of national objectives and performs peacetime missions that are compatible with training and mobilization readiness requirements. Responsibilities include airlift and refueling duties. The command also provides functional mission support units, including aerial port operations, civil engineering, security forces, intelligence, military training, communications, mobility support, combat logistics support, transportation and services.

Operation Recognition

Operation Recognition is a program of the Riverside County Board of Education, with assistance from the Riverside County Department of Veterans' Services. Residents of Riverside who missed completing high school due to military service in World War II, the Korean War or the Vietnam War, or due to internment in World War II Japanese-American relocation camps, may receive high school diplomas awarded by Operation Recognition at ceremonies held periodically throughout the year. Family members may submit applications to recognize qualifying individuals posthumously.

Above: The March Field Air Museum has an extensive collection. *Author's photo.*

Left: A bomber pilot bust by artist Don Winton, dedicated to the courageous airmen who piloted the bombers that turned the tide of World War II. *Author's photo.*

Standing since 1999 outside the March Field Air Museum is a Minuteman II missile. *Author's photo.*

Qualifications for a diploma require that the applicant or recipient be a Riverside County resident or, if a veteran, that they provide proof of honorable discharge from the U.S. military during World War II (service December 7, 1941–December 31, 1946), the Korean War (service June 27,

The gift shop at the museum has a wide assortment of aviation mementos. *Author's photo.*

1950–January 31, 1955) or the Vietnam War (service August 5, 1964–May 7, 1975), or from February 28, 1961, for veterans who served in country before August 5, 1964.

Japanese-American citizens must show proof of internment in a World War II relocation camp. Persons who meet qualifications but earned GEDs are eligible.

In 1980, the March Field Museum was recognized as a U.S. Air Force facility and opened to the public.

That same year, the March Field Museum Foundation was established. The March Field Museum Foundation, with nearly one thousand supporters, is now solely responsible for maintaining and displaying approximately five thousand museum items and aircraft on loan from the U.S. Air Force. All air force financial contributions ended on April 1, 1996, when the March Air Force Base was realigned.

The foundation is a nonprofit organization dedicated to the support of the museum.

In 1993, the museum moved to its current location in a 26,880-square-foot facility on the west side of the runway. In 1999, the name of the museum was changed to the March Field Air Museum.

Representative Ken Calvert's bill HR 320 for the Distinguished Flying Cross Memorial at March Air Field Museum was passed overwhelmingly by the House of Representative on October 24, 2011. *Author's photo.*

The Nation Distinguished Flying Cross Memorial is dedicated to all those heroic aviators who have earned the Distinguished Flying Cross. *Author's photo.*

Over seventy historic aircraft are on display both inside and outside the main museum building. Many famous record-breaking planes such as the Lockheed SR-71 Blackbird are represented, as are the strategic bombers and fighters of the cold war period. World War II is well represented by planes such as the B-17 Flying Fortress, the B-25 Mitchell bomber, the Douglas A/B-26 Invader and the magnificent B-29 Superfortress. Inside, the visitor will find some rare and unusual aircraft, including a P-59 fighter, the first operational jet adopted by the U.S. Air Force over fifty years ago.

Nose Art

Fine examples of nose art can be seen at the March Field Air Museum. Nose art is a decorative painting or design on the fuselage of a military aircraft, usually located near the nose, and is a form of aircraft graffiti. While it was begun for practical reasons, the practice evolved to express the individuality often constrained by the uniformity of the military. Men at war sought a way to personalize the planes to recall more peaceful times. Some nose art helped to identify particular squadrons, such as the Flying Tigers. In general, nose art provided a way for individualizing the planes that went off to combat. In a way, nose art was a talisman to provide protection from the stress of war. Because it was never officially approved, nose art was considered to be a wartime type of folk art. The artists of most nose art often remain anonymous.

One example of nose art at March is the North American B-25J Mitchell. This extremely versatile bomber was built by North American Aviation at its Kansas City, Kansas plant. The North American B-25 Mitchell is named in honor of Brigadier General William "Billy" Mitchell, who pioneered the concept of strategic aerial bombardment.

In April 1942, Lieutenant Colonel James H. "Jimmy" Doolittle, later lieutenant general, led one of the most daring missions of the war flying the B-25. Only five months after the surprise attack on Pearl Harbor, Lieutenant Colonel Doolittle led sixteen B-25 Mitchell bombers off the deck of the USS *Hornet*. The B-25s bombed Tokyo, Yokohama, Kobe and Nagoya. Lieutenant Colonel Doolittle's "Tokyo Raiders" were successful in their mission. The museum received this aircraft by truck in 1982. It was restored in 1998, wearing colors of the Forty-second Bomb Group, Thirteenth Air Force, and was named Problem Child. The attack was depicted in words and in the movie *Thirty Seconds Over Tokyo* starring Spencer Tracy as Jimmy Doolittle.

The practice of nose art was initiated during World War I. Italian and German pilots painted pictures on the noses of their planes before going into combat. In 1913, the first nose art was found on an Italian flying boat. The image was that of a large sea monster. Famed Italian pilot Francesco Baracca had a prancing horse painted on the front of his plane.

During World War I, the United States Ninety-fourth Aero Squadron had the art of the "Hat in the Ring" on the front of its airplanes.

One of the most well-known nose art designs was the shark face painting made popular by the American Flying Tigers.

Although the roots of nose art date back to World War I, the nose art of World War II has been highly praised for the embellished designs considered by many to be the golden age of nose art. During World War II, many Axis and Allied pilots flew planes with nose art displayed on the front.

Some nose art honored female movie stars popular in the day, such as Betty Grable; the nose art on the B-29 Superfortress honored Ernie Pyle.

A popular design during World War II was the famous "Dragon and His Tail." This design was painted on the B-24J Liberator or the United States Air Force Fifth, Sixty-fourth Bomb Squadron, Forty-third Bomb Group, in the South Pacific. The design encompassed the entire length of the plane.

One well-known nose art artist was Tony Starcer, who painted hundreds of B-17s. One of the designs was known as the "Memphis Belle."

Nose art declined after the Korean War.

During the Vietnam War, squadrons and planes were often named after the art that graced the noses of their planes. Popular themes were Thor, the Angel of Death, Ghost Rider and War Lord.

Nose art continued to surface during Operation Desert Storm, Operation Enduring Freedom and Operation Iraqi Freedom.

The museum features many aircraft on display, both inside and outside its walls. Aircraft that were on display as of July 2012 are (alphabetically):

A-26C (Invader), Douglas
A-37 (Dragonfly), Cessna
A-7D (Corsair II), LTV
AH-1F (Cobra), Bell
An-2 (Colt), PZL Mielec, model 1975
B-17G (Flying Fortress), Boeing
B-25J (Mitchell), North American

B-29A (Superfortress), Boeing
B-47E (Stratojet), Boeing
B-52D (Stratofortress), Boeing
B-8M Gyrocopter, Benson
BT-13A (Valiant), Vultee
BT-13A, Vultee (Japanese D-3 Val replica)
C-119G (Flying Boxcar), Fairchild
C-123K (Provider), Fairchild
C-131D (Samaritan), Convair
C-141B (Starlifter), Lockheed
C-45J (Expediter), Beech
C-54Q (Skymaster), Douglas (Navy)
CT-39A (Sabreliner), North American
D-21 Drone (for Blackbird program), Lockheed
EA-1E, Douglas
EB-57B (Canberra), Martin
F-100C (Super Sabre), North American
F-101B (Voodoo), McDonnell-Douglas
F-102A (Delta Dagger), Convair
F-104 (Starfighter), Lockheed
F-105B (Thunderchief), Republic
F-105D (Thunderchief), Republic
F-15, McDonnell-Douglas
F-4C (Phantom II), McDonnell-Douglas
F-4E (Phantom II), McDonnell-Douglas
F-84C (Thunderjet), Republic
F-84F (Thunderstreak), Republic
F-86H (Sabre), North American
F-86L (Sabre), North American
F-89J (Scorpion), Northrop
FB-111A (Aardvark), General Dynamics
FO-141 (Gnat), Folland
H-21B (Workhorse), Piasecki
HU-16E (Albatross), Grumman
KC-135A (Stratotanker), Boeing
KC-97L (Stratofreighter), Boeing
L-5 (Sentinel), Stinson
MiG-15 (Fagot), Mikoyan-Gurevich (side painted fuselage number 273)
MiG-17 (Fresco), Mikoyan-Gurevich (side painted fuselage number 1605)

MiG-19 (Farmer), Mikoyan-Gurevich (side painted fuselage number 0409)
MiG-21F-13 (Fishbed C), Mikoyan-Gurevich (side painted fuselage number 1101)
MiG-23BN (Flogger H), Mikoyan-Gurevich (side painted fuselage number 5744)
O-2B (Super Skymaster), Cessna
OH-6A (Cayuse), Hughes
P-38L (Lightning), Lockheed, Fiberglass replica
P-39Q (Airacobra), Bell
P-59A (Airacomet), Bell
PT-13D, Stearman note: this was originally built as a PT-17
PT-19B (Cornell), Fairchild
PT-6A, Consolidated
R50-5 (Lodestar), Lockheed
Replica (7/8 scale) P-6 (Hawk), Curtiss
Replica, Nieuport 11 (7/8 scale), Nieuport
RF-4C (Phantom II), McDonnell-Douglas
SNJ-4 (Texan), North American
SR-71A (Blackbird), Lockheed
T-33A (Shooting Star), Lockheed
T-37B (Tweet), Cessna
T-38A (Talon), Northrop
TA4J (Skyhawk), McDonnell-Douglas
TG-2 Glider, Schweizer
U-9A (Aero Commander), Rockwell
UH-1F (Iroquois), Bell
VC-47A (Skytrain), Douglas
YA-9A, Northrop
YF-14A (Tomcat), Grumman

The museum also has a fine display to honor dogs that have served. The War Dog Memorial, dedicated in 2000, honors over three hundred Vietnam, Korea and World War II dogs and their handlers. It is informative to view the great job these dogs have done for the United States. Future plans include the establishment of a memorial for women in aviation in the courtyard of the museum.

PERRIS VALLEY AIRPORT

FAA Identifier:	L65
Lat./Long.:	33-45-52.7000N / 117-13-08.4000W
	33-45.878333N / 117-13.140000W
	33.7646389 / -117.2190000 (estimated)
Elevation:	1413 ft. / 431 m (estimated)
Variation:	14E (1985)
From City:	1 mile SE of PERRIS, CA
Time Zone:	UTC -7 (UTC -8 during Standard Time)
Zip Code:	92570

The Early Days

The Perris Valley Historical Museum shared a wealth of information about the early days of the Perris Valley Airport. In 1952, Al and Lettie Hoyt purchased 120 acres of farmland with the hopes of retirement and with the ability to have their own runway. Unfortunately, this dream was not a reality. At one time, the Hoyts owned a Short Wing Piper. The Hoyts leased the land to two crop-dusters, Gerald Kiernan and Karl Christiansen. By 1961, Kiernan had graded and oiled the runway and obtained an operating permit from the Riverside County Planning Commission. He also started a skydiving operation at the airport.

In the early 1960s, when Perris Airport was in its infancy, a commercial artist by the name of Harvey Ball was given the task of creating a design for the employees at State Mutual Life Assurance Company. He created the design of a yellow circle with two round dots for the eyes and a curved half circle for the mouth. The smiley face design quickly spread around the world.

When Perris was in its infancy, the record was set for two hours, forty-seven minutes for a flight from Ontario, California, to New York at speeds up to 869 miles per hour. This was a huge difference from the early days of aviation and the barnstormers who took close to a month to travel across the United States.

In Perris, California, parachuting was introduced as a new sport in Riverside County. At the same time in the United States, a gallon of gas was selling for twenty-seven cents, and the cost of buying a house was $12,500.

In 1961, the estimate of the world population reached 4.00 billion. The world population is the sum total of all living humans on earth. As of 2012, it is estimated by the United States Census Bureau to number 7.03 billion.

By 1965, the airport had been licensed by both the Federal Aviation Administration (FAA) and the State Division of Aeronautics. In 1971, Kiernan and Paul Finnell took over the management of the airport. Time

Aerial view of Skydive Perris. *Courtesy of Melanie Peschio and the Conatser family.*

passed, and Bill and Lyndelle "Lindy" Meyers took over the lease; eventually, in the 1970s, the Meyerses bought the land from the Hoyts. The Hoyts eventually settled in Apple Valley. Lindy Meyers died in Cottage Grove, Oregon, in 2003. Lindy's husband, Bill, had preceded her years earlier.

In 1976, the Conatser family purchased the Perris Valley Airport and has kept it as a family owned and operated business over the years. Through the years, both the business and the sport of skydiving have grown. In 1989, the Conastsers' children, Pat and Melanie, took over the operation of the airport and the growing skydiving business.

The Conatser Family

The Conatsers have a true family operation, with all members taking a role.

Bennie (Ben) Ernest Conatser

Bennie is the husband, father, grandfather, brother and co-owner of the Perris Valley Airport, along with his wife, Diane. Ben has 1,600 hours as a PIC (pilot in command) in aircraft like his World War I Fokker Tri-plane, his Merlin and his privately owned DC-9, which has been modified for skydiving. Also, Ben has accumulated 10,000 hours as a flight engineer for a commercial airline (Oversea's National Airways [ONA]), flying a DC-10, prior to purchasing the airport in 1976. Ben still flies and maintains his advanced license, IA (inspection authorization) and A&P (airframe and power plant) mechanic rating today at the age of seventy. Ben has always been a man of accomplishments that most wouldn't even attempt. His inner strength, work ethic and love for his family are undeniable.

Patricia "Diane" Conatser

Patricia is the wife, mother, grandmother and co-owner of the Perris Valley Airport, along with husband Ben. Diane is also an aviator, with three hundred flight hours in small tail-dragger airplanes like the Cessna 140 and 170. Prior to purchasing the airport, Diane used to fly her then young children around as their second mode of transportation. Diane also has made two tandem skydives. Most people know Diane as one of the sweetest women they'll ever meet and as the life of any party. Her close friends and family also know her as a very smart woman, with great vision and tenacity and a kindness that is second to none.

Ben and Diane, together from 1976 until turning the business over to their kids in 1989, showed true dedication and years of tireless effort to create a strong and reputable skydiving center that has become world-renowned.

Their kids, Patrick and Melanie, began purchasing the family business in 1989 and are still running the largest skydiving center in the world as of this writing. The business was included in a time capsule in May 2011.

Patrick Merle Conatser

Pat is the father, son, brother and co-owner of Perris Valley Aviation Services, Skydive Perris, Perris Valley Skydiving School, PM Leasing and the Bombshelter Restaurant & Bar, with his sister and business partner, Melanie Peschio. Pat has 3,000 flight hours as a PIC (pilot in command) of many aircraft, such as his private Cessna 180, three Twin Otters, two Shorts Brothers Skyvans, the Fokker Tri-plane and the family DC-9. Pat also worked for the airlines "Total Air" as a flight engineer and accumulated 3,500 hours. Pat, with his A&P rating, oversees the maintenance for the aircraft and flies the Skydive Perris planes. Pat has eighty-nine skydives, most of which were round parachute jumps in the 1980s, when skydiving was dangerous and sex was safe. Pat's biggest passion over and above airplanes is his love for Corvettes.

Melanie Conatser-Peschio

Melanie is wife to John Peschio, stepmom to Mathew Peschio, mother to dog Gracie and cats Clyde and Samantha, daughter, sister, aunt to Ryan Conatser and co-owner of Perris Valley Aviation Services, Skydive Perris, Perris Valley Skydiving School, PM Leasing and the Bombshelter Restaurant & Bar, with her brother and business partner, Patrick Conatser. Melanie is the skydiver of the family, with 5,500 skydives, many world records and other amazing skydiving experiences accumulated over twenty years. Melanie also is a private pilot with 150 flight hours. Melanie commented, "I would like to say, about myself, that I have a genuine kindness to all mankind and that I have a special love for animals. I truly feel grateful that I have not only grown up with my family, but have grown old with them too…we are so very fortunate but have worked very hard together to get there!"

John Peschio

John is Melanie's husband and a pilot for Southwest Airlines, with twelve thousand flight hours and 4,500 skydives. John's son lives in Colorado and is nineteen years old.

Ryan Patrick Conatser

Ryan, son to Patrick Conatser, was eleven years old in July 2012. Ryan is the new light of the Conatser family, and they will do everything they can to instill great values in him and support him in whatever path his life will take. Most of all, he will continue the Conatser family morals. It is likely that Ryan will carry on the family business.

The airport's location is unique in that it is surrounded by wide-open land, with approximately six hundred acres and relatively unrestricted airspace. The airport itself is on eighty-five privately owned acres, fifteen acres of which can strictly be used to service and support any military program with separate air/jump operations.

Skydive Perris is within a reasonable distance from majorly populated areas. It is thirty-five miles south of Ontario International Airport, seventy-five miles southeast of Los Angeles Airport, seventy-five miles north of San Diego Airport and nine miles south of March Air Reserve Base.

In 2011, and for the past thirty-five years, Skydive Perris has been a leader in the skydiving industry. In addition to the sport aspect, for the last decade various U.S. military units, as well as foreign militaries, have begun utilizing some civilian skydiving centers to conduct their training. Skydive Perris has become the training location of choice for much military training because of its ability to provide military units with aircraft, facilities and one of only two on-site wind tunnels in the world.

There is a full restaurant and bar, rigging services and the equipment and staffing needed in order to train efficiently, effectively and safely.

1-800-SKYDIVE
INDOOR
SKYDIVING

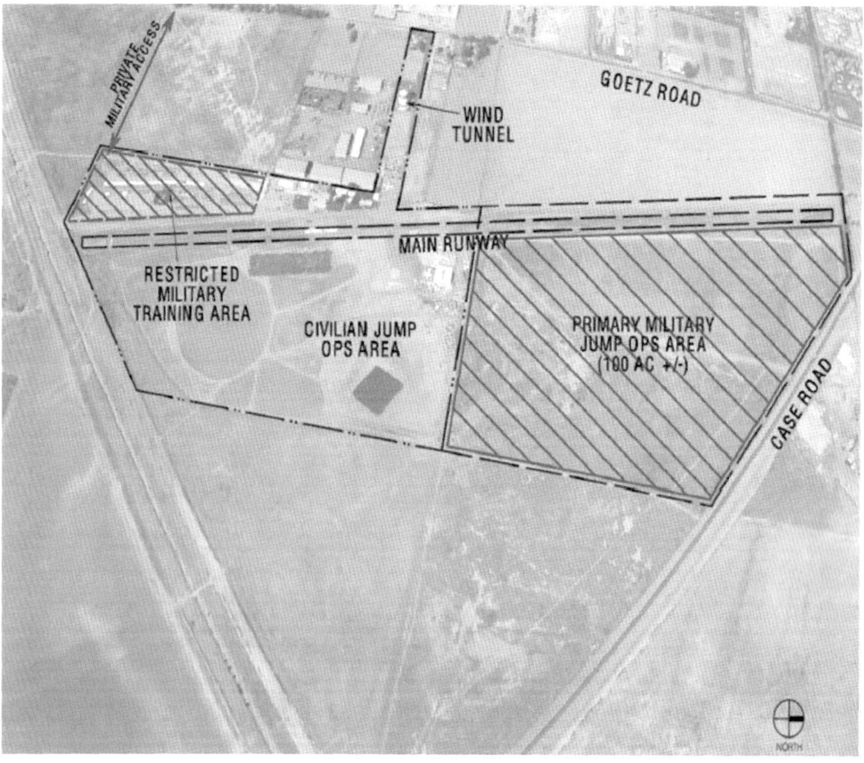
PRIVATE
MILITARY ACCESS
WIND
TUNNEL
GOETZ ROAD
MAIN RUNWAY
RESTRICTED
MILITARY
TRAINING AREA
CIVILIAN JUMP
OPS AREA
PRIMARY MILITARY
JUMP OPS AREA
(100 AC +/-)
CASE ROAD
NORTH

Interior view of the indoor-jump wind tunnel. *Courtesy of Melanie Peschio and the Conatser family.*

Opposite, top: Skydive Perris has become the training location of choice for much military training because of its ability to provide military units with aircraft, facilities and one of only two on-site wind tunnels in the world. *Courtesy of Melanie Peschio and the Conatser family.*

Opposite, bottom: Map showing the combined military and civilian skydiving areas of Skydive Perris. *Courtesy of Melanie Peschio and the Conatser family.*

Some of the military groups that regularly conduct their training at Skydive Perris include:

U.S. Navy
U.S. Marines
U.S. Army
Royal Navy Royal Marines, England
Royal Artillery, England
Special Forces, Singapore
Special Forces, Sweden
Special Forces, Canada
Qatar Military Forces
UAE Military Forces

DC9, one of the planes used at Skydive Perris. *Courtesy of Melanie Peschio and the Conatser family.*

A jump plane used at Skydive Perris. *Courtesy of Melanie Peschio and the Conatser family.*

Sea Otter plane, used in skydiving at Skydive Perris. *Courtesy of Melanie Peschio and the Conatser family.*

The airport, which is privately owned, is a public-use airport that isn't hindered by any other aviation activity and has maintained a great relationship with the City of Perris.

On average, there are approximately 140,000 total jumps each year, while 10,000 of them are first-time students. Skydive Perris has been a leader in the sport-parachuting industry, hosting four U.S. National Championships, a World Cup and countless World Record events.

Skydive Perris owns and operates three De Havilland Twin Otters, two Shorts Sky Vans, one Pilatus Porter and one DC-9 Jet. All aircraft are maintained on site in accordance with the manufacturer and are FAA approved through the 135-type program, and all routine and non-routine maintenance is performed by FAA certified mechanics.

The airport's most rewarding events (and the family's greatest accomplishments) have been their efforts toward raising money for breast cancer research and awareness. In 2009, the facility set a new world record with a 181-person, all-female skydiving formation. That year alone, Skydive Perris wrote a check for $500,000 to the City of Hope.

Skydive Perris has the unique combination of facilities, expert instructors and experience to exceed the government's expectations for military freefall high-altitude, low-opening/high-altitude, high-opening (HALO/HAHO) sustainment training. Skydive Perris stands ready to support any unit from across the globe. *Courtesy of Melanie Peschio and the Conatser family.*

On average, Skydive Perris makes 140,000 total jumps each year, 10,000 of them first-time students, in addition to hosting four U.S. National Championship and a World Cup event, as well as numerous world record skydiving formations. *Courtesy of Melanie Peschio and the Conatser family.*

All ages can have fun at the indoor-jump wind tunnel. *Courtesy of Melanie Peschio and the Conatser family.*

The facility has now chosen as its charity spinal cord research through the Reeve-Irvine Research Center in Irvine, California. The Conatser family hopes to continue their passion toward reaching out to others in need over the next decade.

Skydive Perris has been chosen as a destination for movies, commercials and celebrities.

Some notable first-time jumpers have included Sean Penn, David Blaine, Cameron Diaz, Drew Barrymore, Patrick Swayze (and Don Swayze), Bob Burnquist, Matt Hoffman (X-Games BMX champ), Tony Hawk, George Bush and Michelle Rodriguez.

Commercials have included Energizer, Bud Light and California Lottery.

Movies have included *The Bucket List*, *Iron Man*, *Jane Austen Book Club* (Melanie Conatser Peschio was a stunt double in it) and *Shoot 'Em Up*.

Television shows have included: *America's Next Top Model*, MTV's *Next* and *Parental Control*, *Stunt Junkies* and *Unsolved History*.

RIVERSIDE MUNICIPAL AIRPORT

FAA Identifier:	RAL
Lat./Long.:	33-57-06.8000N / 117-26-42.4000W
	33-57.113333N / 117-26.706667W
	33.9518889 / -117.4451111 (estimated)
Elevation:	819 ft. / 249.6 m (surveyed)
Variation:	14E (2000)
From City:	4 miles SW of RIVERSIDE, CA
Time Zone:	UTC -8 (UTC -7 during Daylight Saving Time)
Zip Code:	92504

Early Days

The current Riverside Municipal Airport was established as a dirt strip in the town of Arlington. It was originally called Arlington Airport. The city of Riverside annexed Arlington in 1961, and in 1964, the airport became known as Riverside Arlington Airport. The neighborhood of Arlington, located about five miles southwest of downtown Riverside, was first settled in the 1870s. It was developed as a farm by Samuel C. Evans and William Sayward. Citrus groves flourished in the area, providing the community with a newfound wealth. Arlington's commercial district at Van Buren

Boulevard and Magnolia Avenue expanded to include a bank, the chamber of commerce, a newspaper, a store, a church, a boardinghouse and a post office with its own Arlington postmark, in use since 1888. In the early 1900s, an electric railway was built down the center of Magnolia Avenue, ending at beautiful Chemewa Park.

Clarence Prest

Clarence O. Prest established an aircraft company in the town of Arlington in the 1920s. Clarence built some of his airplanes in the old lemon packinghouse at the corner of Van Buren and Indiana Streets in Arlington, California. *Courtesy of Tony Haraman, http://earlyaviators.com/eprest.htm.*

The Arlington Airport was used as early as the 1920s. Clarence O. Prest established an aircraft company in the town of Arlington in the 1920s. Prest built some of his airplanes in the old lemon packinghouse at the corner of Van Buren and Indiana Streets.

Prest's small exhibition plane, Poison, was shipped to Las Vegas by rail late in November 1920. He put on a demonstration, but unfortunately the motor stopped, causing the airplane to plunge to the ground from a height of seventy-five feet; luckily, the pilot was uninjured. The motor stopped because the castor oil that was used for lubricating the rotary engine was carelessly put in the gasoline tank.

Prest and Loyal Morton Bach, a relative of the composer, built a small plane named the Polar Bear. Prest later attempted to fly it from Mexico to Siberia but landed instead in Ketchikan, Alaska. In later life, Prest returned to California and owned an airplane surplus business. He lost the business during the Depression. During World War

Prest's small exhibition plane, Poison, was shipped to Las Vegas by rail late in November 1920. He put on a demonstration flight during which the airplane plunged to the ground from a height of seventy-five feet. The motor stopped, and the Poison poked its nose into the ground with considerable force, doing some damage to the machine. Mr. C.O. Prest, owner and pilot of the plane, escaped with a slight shaking up. *Courtesy of Tony Haraman, http://earlyaviators.com/eprest.htm.*

Exterior of Riverside Municipal Airport. The current Riverside Municipal Airport was established as a dirt strip in the town of Arlington. It was originally called Arlington Airport. When the city of Riverside annexed Arlington, the airport became known as Riverside Arlington Airport. *Author's photo.*

II, he developed a process for speeding up production on airplane parts by using templates. He died in 1954 at the age of fifty-eight.

Little is known of the facility in the 1930s. However, it did survive the war to become a thriving business in the city. The *Arlington Times* reported in October 1939 that an aviation instructor from Florida named L.H. Slaughter purchased the facility. The airport was closed during World War II because private flying was restricted.

Albert Des Mazes took over Arlington Airport in June 1941. In 1946, Karl A. Gemende took over the management of the airport. By 1950, the facility had grown to nineteen acres, and thirty-five additional acres were leased. In 1951, Eugene Best, a lawyer and pilot, took action to preserve the field and expand it as a flying center. Today, Gemende Drive is adjacent to the airport. In 1952, the airport was purchased by the City of Riverside and became Riverside Municipal Airport.

The 1950s

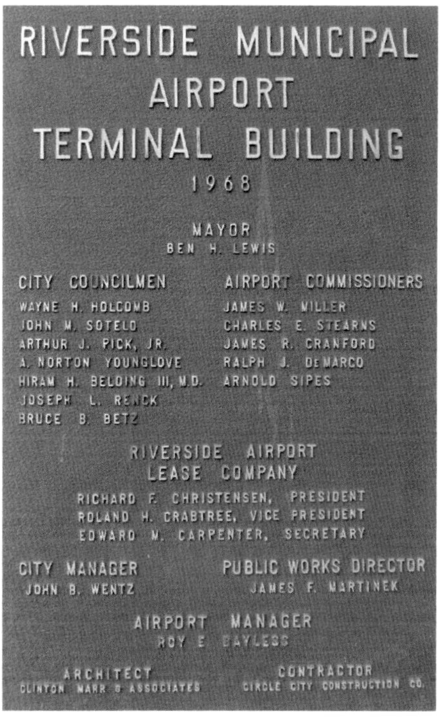

The current Riverside Municipal Airport terminal building was dedicated in 1968. *Author's photo.*

In aviation history, the world's first passenger jet, the Comet, was produced in the United Kingdom in the early 1950s, signaling the start of faster and cheaper air travel in later years.

There were big differences in 1952 compared to the time when Prest was involved at the airport in Arlington in the 1920s. In the 1920s, a loaf of bread cost nine cents, a dozen eggs cost forty-four cents, a gallon of gasoline cost twenty-two cents and the average price for a new car was $265;

however, in the 1950s, a new cost the buyer a whopping $1,700, and a home could be purchased for around $9,000.

The FAA provided $500,000 to build a modern runway at the facility. Riverside Municipal Airport was dedicated in 1956.

1970s

In 1975, Riverside Municipal Airport hosted the Twenty-eighth Annual Powder Puff Derby, a race for female pilots as part of the AWTAR (All Woman Transcontinental Air Race, Inc). The year 1947 saw the first of the All-Woman Air Races, from Palm Springs, California, to Tampa, Florida. That year, the race had only two contestants; the next year, there were seven. The 1948 and 1949 Jacqueline Cochran All-Woman Transcontinental Air Races (AWTAR) were the formal beginning of what would become popularly known as the Powder Puff Derby, a reference to the 1929 Women's Air Derby by humorist and aviation advocate Will Rogers.

The first Women's Air Derby on August 13–20, 1929, was a transcontinental race as part of the National Air Races at Cleveland and was entered by twenty female flyers. At the time, there were only seventy U.S.-licensed female pilots, but only forty met the race requirements of having one hundred hours of solo flight, including twenty-five hours of solo cross-country, a license from the Federation Aeronautique Internationale (FAI) and an annual sporting license issued by the National Aeronautics Association (NAA). Of that group, there were twenty entrants in the derby.

It took eight days to fly and navigate the route using only dead reckoning and road maps. Louise Thaden came in first, and fourteen others who completed the race in one of the two aircraft categories were Amelia Earhart, Ruth Elder, Edith Foltz, Mary Haizlip, Jessie Keith-Miller, Opal Kunz, Blanche Noyes, Gladys O'Donnell, Phoebe Omlie, Neva Paris, Thea Rasche and Bobbi Trout.

In contrast, the 1975 Riverside air race required a local Ninety-Nines Chapter to accept the task to organize the coast-to-coast race. The Ninety-Nines, Inc., is an international organization of licensed female pilots from thirty-five countries. The organization has thousands of members throughout the world. The international headquarters is located in Oklahoma City, Oklahoma. Although there are other female pilot organizations in various

Above: The air show at Riverside Municipal Airport is an annual family-fun event. *Author's photo.*

Left: The Riverside Municipal Airport has been holding air shows for the past twenty years, starting in 1992. *Author's photo.*

states and nations, virtually all women of achievement in aviation have been or are members of the Ninety-Nines.

In 1974–75, female pilots from the Riverside area banded together to form the new Inland California Chapter. The year before, Riverside had been slated to host the air race; however, the race was canceled "as a result of the energy crunch." The race was represented in many newspapers across the country. The wife and mother-in-law of Charles Schulz, creator of the *Peanuts* comic strip, entered the race and were featured in *Peanuts* as Peppermint Patty and Marci, flying with Snoopy's Sopwith Camel (aka his doghouse).

For the past twenty years, the facility has hosted the annual Riverside Air Show, which draws thousands of onlookers.

Commemorative Air Force

The Commemorative Air Force Inland Empire chapter is located in a hangar at Riverside Municipal Airport and has provided years of dedicated service to the Riverside Air Show.

The Inland Empire Squadron was founded in 1989. At that time, it was located in Rialto, California, and was not doing very well. A group from Corona, California, took it over and moved the headquarters to the Corona Airport. The four members who were responsible for this action were Art Seidler, Lyle Page, Bob Hemborg and Don Helms. *Author's photo.*

The first plane assigned to the squadron was the L-4F in 1991 and then the Ryan PT-22 in 1992. The squadron moved to the Riverside Airport in 1994 and became the Inland Empire Wing. Today, it has approximately eighty-seven members. *Author's photo.*

CAF IEW C-53D air and ground crew group picture. *Courtesy of Pete Downes.*

Opposite, bottom: The Commemorative Air Force (CAF) is an all-volunteer organization made up of members from all walks of life. Membership is open to all men and women age eighteen or older. *Author's photo.*

The Commemorative Air Force (CAF) is an all-volunteer organization made up of members from all walks of life. Membership is open to all men and women age eighteen or older. You need not be a veteran or a pilot to join the CAF. Privately funded and totally self-supporting, the nonprofit, tax-exempt group is dedicated to preserving the military aviation heritage of World War II. In the late 1950s, Lloyd Nolen and a few other pilots joined together and purchased a P-51 Mustang. Their pleasure in restoration and maintaining the old plane soon grew into an international organization. The first Commemorative Air Force was established as a nonprofit organization in Texas with the goal of preserving World War II combat aircraft. During World War II, the United States had produced close to 300,000 planes, but within a few brief years, most of the World War II war birds were out of sight. The motto of the CAF is "Keep 'Em Flying!"

The Inland Empire Chapter was founded in 1989. At that time, it was located in Rialto, California, but did not do very well. A group from Corona, California, took it over and moved the headquarters to the Corona Airport.

The four members who were responsible for this action were Art Seidler, Lyle Page, Bob Hemborg and Don Helms.

The first plane assigned to the squadron was the L-4F in 1991 and then the Ryan PT-22 in 1992. The squadron moved to the Riverside Airport in 1994 and became the Inland Empire Wing. Today, there are approximately eighty-seven members.

SKYLARK FIELD AIRPORT

FAA Identifier:	CA89
Lat./Long.:	33-37-48.0810N / 117-18-06.1360W
	33-37.801350N / 117-18.102267W
	33.6300225 / -117.3017044 (estimated)
Elevation:	1253 ft. / 382 m (estimated)
Variation:	14E (1985)
From City:	4 miles S of LAKE ELSINORE, CA
Time Zone:	UTC -7 (UTC -8 during Standard Time)
Zip Code:	92530

Skylark Field Airport has one major business: Skydive Lake Elsinore, also commonly called Lake Elsinore DZ. It has one of the longest histories in U.S. jumping history and probably more owners than any other in the country. The land itself was once called Laguna Grande by Mexico and was part of a Mexican land grant. The land was purchased in 1883 for $24,000.

The history of Skylark Air Field started in 1954, when Forest "Cy" Perkins and his wife, Florence Perkins, purchased approximately 190 acres of land in Lake Elsinore. The land was purchased from the Elsinore Naval and Military School and was first known as the Gordon Hunt Airport.

Cy and Florence Perkins first got involved in aviation in the late 1920s, when they worked at Travel Air and Stearman Aircraft Company in Wichita, Kansas. They later worked for TWA and Rearwin Aircraft companies. In

This photo shows the wide-open, unobstructed space at Skylark Field. *Author's photo.*

1934, they moved to California. After coming to California, they worked for Douglas Aircraft in Santa Monica. It wasn't long before Cy, Florence and Cy's brother, Bill, started Skylark Manufacturing Company. The company made landing gear, motor mounts and sheet metal for World War II aircraft. At one time, the company employed close to two hundred people.

After World War II, the Perkinses continued to manufacture various parts for aircraft. When they moved to Lake Elsinore, they started Skylark Aviation.

Cy's original plan was to do manufacturing on the land. The airfield had two dirt runways and a concrete slab that measured twenty by thirty feet. Perkins had a manufacturing facility in Venice, California, that built airplane parts. The airport, which was built from scratch, evolved into a leading facility for jumpers and soaring.

When Cy purchased the land for Skylark Field in 1954, Lake Elsinore was completely dry. There were tall tales about a marine monster that lived in the lake. The Elsinore Valley exists today because of water. Since the Lake Elsinore area is located in a desert region, early settlers made do with scarce local water resources. Life was hard.

In 1954, the yearly inflation rate in the United States was 0.32 percent, the average cost of a new house was $10.250, the cost of a gallon of gas

Interior of a jump plane used at Skylark. *Author's photo.*

Exterior of a jump plane used at Skylark. *Author's photo.*

was twenty-two cents, the average cost of a new car was $1,700, the average monthly rent was $85, a movie ticket was seventy cents and *Life* magazine was twenty cents. Also in 1954, Armistice Day was renamed Veterans' Day to honor the veterans from the Civil War, World War I, World War II and the Korean conflict.

A year later, in 1955, the city of Lake Elsinore became public property for the first time in its history. Voters approved a $1.6 million bond issue for the construction of the 112,000-foot loop line around the lake, the Canyon Lake Water Treatment Plant and the Lakeview Siphon, the point of connection to the Metropolitan Water District through the Western Metropolitan Water District (WMWD) facilities.

By the mid-1960s, the Perkinses were able to grow the collection of planes to eight, including two Aeroncas for training (one was also used for towing gliders). They also had a Cessna 172 for hauling parachute jumpers, a Cessna 180 for jumpers, a Callair and a glider. They were able to construct two large hangars, a trailer court and a weekend snack bar.

Filming at Skylark

Within five years after buying the property, it was famous for soaring and skydiving. The show *Man and the Challenge* was filmed at Skylark. The show was a thirty-six-segment, half-hour television adventure/science fiction series that ran new episodes on NBC from September 12, 1959, to June 11, 1960. It starred George Nader as Dr. Glenn Barton, a research scientist for the Institute of Human Factors, an agency that conducted experiments designed to measure human endurance for the United States government. The series was produced by Ivan Tors. Nader's costars included Jack Ging as Dan Wright, Michael Masters as Bill Locke, the Canadian-born Joyce Meadows as Lynn Allen and Michael Keith as Matt Adams. The episodes focused on various individuals setting world records of strength, endurance and mastery of various difficult skills. The program also featured appearances by Bethel Leslie as Eleanor Beck in "The Early Warning," Ted Knight as Dr. Herter in the episode "Daredevils" and Raymond Bailey in the role of Dr. Kramer in the series opener "The Sphere of No Return." Joining Knight in that segment was Paul Burke.

During the 1950s through the 1970s, Skylark Field Airport was home to several soaring schools. In 1976, Perkins sold the airport.

In the early 1960s, Elsinore was operated by Dave Burt's Para Ventures. Burt was a paratrooper in the United States Air Force in the 1940s. He then became a smoke jumper for the U.S. Forestry Service. Next he made a career switch and began movie stunt work and exhibition jumping. Jim Hall was his partner. Hall left the air force at the end of World War II as a flight engineer and pilot. They started Para Ventures, the first parachute-jumping business operated in the world. Burt and Hall made jumps at sporting events, fairs and rodeos, bringing more attention to the sport and their business.

Hall's jumping and sense of adventure took him to Mexico, where he did parachuting exploration, looking for the lost gold mines of the Spanish conquistadors. Often, his jumping companion was his pit bull/boxer mix, Ace.

Hall was doing a jump for a commercial when he landed in the water next to a party yacht instead of the beach in Acapulco, Mexico. The people on the boat pulled Hall onboard. It was then that he met a Hollywood movie producer. Because of this unplanned circumstance, Hall had the opportunity to meet Marvin Greenberg. The two had a lengthy conversation. Hall agreed to write a script for an adventure show about jumping. The idea was sold to Ivan Tors Films in association with ZIV–United Artists Television. Burt and Hall selected the jumpers who would participate in the show. The jumpers included Bob Henry, Bud Kiesow, Vern Williams and Bob Sinclair. The action was captured in black and white in the first season. The popular show *Ripcord* was born. It was later filmed in color. The show starred Larry Pennell as Ted McKeever, Ken Curtis as Jim Buckley and Charlie Kern as the pilot. The original pilot for the series was Chuck Lambert.

TV Show Ripcord

Cameras were mounted on helmets to capture the action. It was a new field, and there was a lot of experimenting to get just the right shots. A lot of the show was filmed in Lake Elsinore at Skylark Field. The show ran for three seasons. The parachutes were mostly from World War II surplus, with modifications made. Panels were removed providing the jumpers with more landing and directional control.

The show aired from 1961 to 1963. The storyline for the show was that the operators of a skydiving company called Ripcord had many exciting adventures and were able to chase bad guys by performing daring rescues. In one episode, there was a fistfight between two characters in midair. The scene was shot by a cameraman who was in freefall with the actors. This series inspired the first widespread interest in parachuting as a sport. Old episodes of *Ripcord* can be found on YouTube.

As a result of the television show, a small toy was made in the 1960s. The small child's toy had a plastic figure with a parachute attached. The idea was to toss the toy into the air and watch it float back down.

In the 1960s, Skylark Field was also the home of the country's only para-scuba club. The club had over two hundred members. This is a sport that combines parachute jumping with scuba diving.

In May 1963, the All-Western Sport Parachute Contest was held at Skylark Field. Hank Simbro was the overall winner of the event. The contest, which was sponsored by Los Angeles Sky Divers, had record crowds and participants. Events included "spot jumping," in which a jumper was required to land from nine to fourteen inches from a target. Another event was a team jump event that required a team of three to jump from 5,500 feet. There was an all-women's event from a jump of 7,500 feet. During the two-day event, a total of 676 jumps were made.

Skydiving was actually begun in the late 1700s by a Frenchman named André-Jacques Garnerin. Jacques flew hot-air balloons before he successfully made the first jump with a silk parachute attached to a basket. He would travel across Europe, floating three thousand feet in the sky above the crowds, cutting the balloon free and falling in the makeshift basket-parachute, doing stunts and antics to scare and amaze the crowd. At the same time, he helped to start the modern-day sport of skydiving.

Skylark Field has been used for several movies and television shows besides the 1960s television show *Ripcord*. Recently, it has been seen in the Windows Phone 7 and commercials for Advanced Auto Parts.

The airport was sold in 1976. There was indication that there were plans to open a large multipurpose sport aviation center with flying, gliding, ballooning and skydiving. These plans never became a reality.

In the 1960s, Larry Perkins was a member of the Eighty-second Airborne Division Sport Parachute Club stationed at Fort Bragg, North Carolina. He made demonstration jumps at Turner Air Force Base and Stewart Air Force Base in Georgia. After his military service, he returned to Skylark Field.

Larry Perkins, the son of Cy Perkins, continues to remain on the property and performs aircraft maintenance and annual aircraft inspections from his

Larry Perkins, son of Skylark Field founder Forest "Cy" Perkins and Florence Perkins, who purchased approximately 190 acres of land in Lake Elsinore in 1954. *Author's photo.*

repair facility located on a corner of Skylark Field. Skydive Elsinore is used extensively for skydiving.

In late 1979, the airport was leased to Leo Orlowski. The new grand opening was in January 1980, but it wasn't long before Skylark Field was once again threatened by flooding from heavy rains. Orlowski moved his business twelve miles south to Murrieta, to a location called Thompson Field, which was also known as Bear Creek Airfield. Thompson Field was a private airstrip that was once open to Ultralights and recreational aviation. It was described as having a single 2,700-foot dirt runway. Thompson Field was owned by Curt Thompson, a local farmer. Several of the farmers would come and sit in some old couches under the oak trees in the evenings and drink beer. The runway was surrounded by the wild wheat that Curt would harvest and bale for feed. When Skylark Airport flooded, the skydiving operation moved there until the waters receded. It was said that Thompson once offered to sell the property for close to $1 million. When the Jack Nicklaus Golf Course was built, there was a large paved road right up to mid-field, where the property ended. Locals remember it as a fun place where people could do some target shooting and have a picnic.

Floods Come to Skylark

Orlowski kept his operation at Thompson Field for close to nine months. Another flood later forced a move back to Thompson Field for approximately seven months, after which Orlowski moved the operation to Hemet. Thompson Field is now abandoned.

In the 1980s, the rise in fuel prices in California affected all skydiving companies. The floodwaters were also a problem.

Floodwaters come every fifty years, more or less, to the Lake Elsinore area. In 1980, the floodwaters covered the entire airport, hangar and adjacent buildings. The main hangar had over eight feet of water and was eventually removed as a result. It took nearly five years for the floodwaters to recede, and the main runway was eventually put back into service.

Skydive Elsinore's Skydiving School is one of the best training facilities in the world, featuring the newest USPA-approved learning progression programs, the most up-to-date equipment (all equipped with automatic activation devices) and the friendliest USPA instructors.

Skydive Elsinore is also commonly called Lake Elsinore DZ. "DZ" is short for Drop Zone. Skydive Elsinore has been in operation since

Skylark Field in Lake Elsinore. It is a noted location for skydiving. *Author's photo.*

1959. It is the longest-operating skydiving operation in North America. The facility is located approximately one hour away from San Diego and metropolitan Los Angeles. Skydive Elsinore fully supports military parachute operations and training. Skydive Elsinore has over two acres of beautiful green grass conveniently located next to the packing and loading areas. DZ owners Karl Gulledge and John Hamilton carefully look over the plush lawn, bubbling fountains and shade trees. These are unique characteristics of Skydive Elsinore—an enchanting oasis of warmth, in both climate and in hospitality.

Skydivers Over Sixty

In 2006, Skydivers Over Sixty (SOS) held its tenth annual event at Skydive Elsinore. Over fifty jumpers participated. John Hamilton and Karl Gulledge spearheaded the event. Hamilton managed the drop zone, while Gulledge managed the Twin Otter flights. During the four-day event, a film crew from Retirement Living Network (RLTV) documented all aspects of the senior skydivers. It produced a film titled *The Art of Living*, which aired on local television stations. In all, there were fifty-three participants who exceeded 190,000 jumps. The ages of Skydivers Over Sixty jumpers for that historic event ranged from sixty to seventy-five. Its average jumpers have completed 600 to 15,000 jumps, each averaging 3,800 jumps. Participants came from Austria, Peru, Canada, Alaska, Hawaii, California and Florida.

The Emmy-nominated, television award–winning series *The Art of Living*, from RLTV, showcased active seniors to show that there are still achievements to be made after retirement. The stars of this series are adults over fifty who define themselves as artists, community activists and athletes. They embody the spirit of optimism and health that is the foundation of this dynamic series. The no-host format of the series allows each inspiring individual to present him or herself through a documentary-like format, letting each tell his or her unique story as he/she sees fit. One of the participants described the beauty of jumping over Lake Elsinore with the homes blanketing the canyons and foothills and being able to see the slight glimmer of the Pacific Ocean in the distance.

World-Class Facility

Skydive Elsinore is a world-class facility, in full support of military parachute operations and training. With ongoing courtesy and increased proficiency with every group, Skydive Elsinore operates all kinds of military training on site, in the safest environment around. Services available include test operations; freshwater LZ (landing zone) drops; surveyed round parachute static-line low-altitude drops; and exclusive military jump runs and/or planeloads.

Skydive Elsinore is also home to cutting-edge research and development in parachute drop testing. The facility has hosted some of the most unique, spectacular and data-rich drops. Skydive Elsinore is proud to have worked with the following companies in the world of parachute technology, research and development: JPL, Pioneer Aerospace, Airborne Systems, Vertigo Inc., JSAF, Cirrus Aircraft Recovery Systems and more, also serving as an Edwards Air Force Base remote test parachute facility.

The professional pilots on staff have flown numerous groups, including the United States Air Force, the Navy Seals, the United States Army, the United Kingdom's British Royal Army, the United Kingdom's Royal Air Force and many more. Essentially, any training operation can be done at Skydive Elsinore with its aircraft and highly experienced pilots.

ABOUT THE AUTHORS

In 1997, Marge Bitetti earned her master's degree in business management from Webster University. Her undergraduate degree is in radio-TV broadcasting from California State University–Long Beach. In 2003, she completed training at Riverside Community College and earned a certificate in grant writing. Awards include: best reporter and numerous first place awards from the National Federation of Press Women. She has authored several nonfiction books. She has also worked as a ghostwriter for nonfiction books. She currently works as a writing consultant and for businesses and nonprofits in the Inland Empire. She is a member of the Author's Guild.

Tony Bitetti's engineering and quality background contribute to the knowledge of requirements for quality documentation. His familiarity with both IBM and Mac platforms adds to his understanding of various programs available. He has over twenty-two years of experience in quality documentation, including graphic design and desktop publishing, as well as creating, controlling, editing, proofreading and maintaining brochures, newsletters, pamphlets, plans and procedures, specifications and technical manuals.